THE COSMIC WAY

by Michal H. Hall

TABLE OF CONTENTS

INTRODUCTION

{I use the short word "reflective" for beings in the cosmos that have evolved to have enough awareness to reflect in to see themselves and reflect out to see what's around them. We obviously know that we are reflective, but we now also know that there are other reflective beings out there in the cosmos.}

Since I've begun my research, I've found that I cannot fully identify with any religious, humanistic, agnostic, atheist or modern pantheist groups. I certainly appreciate some of the things that they teach and stand for, but not enough to join them. Thus when someone asks me what group I belong to; what I believe; or how there can be any meaning in my life without a religion or a god, it's been difficult to articulate. Only recently have I been able to answer with what I've been searching for and am now passing on to you. It's my hope that you will be someone who can appreciate what is to follow, but even if you're not, give it a try.

I can now say that I believe in what has been called called "The Way" in many of the original writings of the World's religions (but of course it has been called by thousands of other names down through the ages). However most of the people who have touched it and acted it out have not been conscious of its powerful presence as they live real and meaningful lives. The powerful, unifying presence of this unifying cosmic being (which might be called things like "ethic, moral, lifestyle, identity, power, or road") is present in religions, philosophy, poetry and really everything...but we sense it and then ignore it and walk away. I'm not really comfortable giving it a name at all because it's so far beyond us, but I have to call it something.

When I refer to what I will call in this book "The Way", people are often confused, so I reply with something like:

"I believe in a cosmic, moral ethic that brings everything together and can bring us (and all reflective beings) together. It is something which reflective beings must choose if they are to have meaningful lives and survive. It can be witnessed in the basic sense of right and wrong that we learn from some of the original writings of the world's religions and our conscience. We can see it in things like the teachings on ethics and in the morality of love, justice, unity and peace, kindness, decency and goodness. It is the unifying force in the cosmos that brings everything together to become more complex, and it should also be doing this for us as Homo sapiens. However we as reflective beings (with the ability to chose) have ignored this underlying, unifying force to choose something else as we loose our natural joyful and sustainable lives. Instead of The Way, we've chosen a renegade emotion we call things like pride, selfishness, arrogance, or greed, that leaves us miserable and going extinct. Thus we have *two* ethical choices open to us...The Way or pride/greed. One brings us together, while the other tears us apart, and it's clear that we have chosen, and are choosing, the wrong one."

Most people stop me there, and I get a strange mix of responses. Some look sleepy; some get mad, and some turn and walk off...but occasionally someone asks me a question or two. I hope you'll be the latter because for me what I call "The Way" has not only brought my thoughts together; it has also helped me to make sense out of the tangled moral and ethical condition of our time. I feel that a great weight has been lifted, because I can now honestly believe in something that is free of greed, superstition and manipulation...and actually makes sense. I can now see that it's the core of what I've believed all along, which I suspect is true with you.

Both this book and the ones I've written before, are recordings of the evolution of my thought's. I grew up with a father who was a Presbyterian minister and head of the philosophy and religion department at UNCW. Thus I was constantly surrounded by mind-stretching conversations and new ideas. I added to my education with bachelor, master and doctor degrees, and decided to continue that education by serving as a Presbyterian minister. I became a follower of Teilhard de Chardin and did two hour long TV shows on his thought on a PBS station in Richmond and another station in Atlanta. I also hosted a variety of other television programs on the same Atlanta station. While I was in Atlanta, I began a large night shelter for people on the streets, and throughout my ministry I was able to start 7 other organizations to meet human need.

I retired from ministry after 40 years and dedicated myself to the research and study of science in areas such as cosmology, climatology, subatomic theory, psychology, paleontology, sociology, and quite a few others. I also studied world religions and the new translations (still coming out) of their writings. All of this inspired me to write several books including a recently published one called The Absurdity of Pride and the Peace of Humility. In it I talk about how pride, arrogance and greed (that all refer to the same thing) are one deviant emotion that has evolved within us to destroy our ability to live meaningful, peaceful lives, and is now dragging us over the cliff of extinction. All of my books have come from this opportunity to personally evolve when I was given the time to do all of this extensive research.

I also found that as a species we are blocking and escaping the reality of just how deviant and violent we've become with our militarism,war, guns, and accepted violence, that are reflected in our television, movies, video games and warped cultures. We've blocked out and escaped just how sick we really are as we overpopulate, pollute the air, water and land, and destroy the plants and animals to wipe out the Earth's ecosystems that sustain us. We are also blocking out the recently discovered fact that our species is going extinct, as well as the fact that we're miserable and unhappy with ourselves, other people, leaders, nations and existence as a whole. We are totally ignoring that something has gone terribly wrong as we sink into the multitude of escapes that are available to us. Obviously I believe that it's past time for us to wake up, look around, and start finding a way out of this mess.

My study of the World Religions has been helpful to me in understanding that there is an underlying moral ethic within them that should be bringing us together, rather than moving apart. However all religions, like everything else, have been taken over by pride to elicit divisive exclusiveness, comparisons, fears and violence. This is causing even our religions to respond with anger, violence, persecution and war. Still the original teachings and writings of the world's religions have talked about love, forgiveness, humility and peace which have helped us see and understand this unifying, moral ethic that I call "The Way".

{There are only a few religious writings that have never had their original teachings (scriptures) undermined by pride and with its superstitions of various gods or spirits. One of these is called the Tao te Ching (writen in he late fourth century BC), which is the main scripture of Taoism in China. I also recently found from a commentary on the Tao te Ching by Dwayne Dyer that it means "The Way". Because of its likeness to what I also call The Way, I have quoted a few words from it at the beginning of each chapter.}

Music or the smell of good cooking
may make people stop and enjoy.
But words that point to The Way
May seem monotonous and without flavor.
When you look for it, there is nothing to see.
When you listen for it, there is nothing to hear.
When you use it, it is inexhaustible.

Tao te Ching

I. Who We Are

Before talking about The Way, I want to be sure we're more or less on the same page about who we are as a species. Most of what I say will make no sense if you don't know a little about what I think on this subject. So here's what I have evolved to understand through my research.

Each one of us is a tiny spot on a planet, that is a tiny spot in our solar system, that's revolving around a star that is a tiny spot in in our galaxy, that is also a teeny tiny spot in the unknowable, vast cosmos. We now know that the cosmos is so huge that nobody can possibly contemplate how big it is or how many stars and galaxies there are. For instance there are billions of stars with trillions of planets just in our galaxy. The nearest star in our galaxy is Proxima Centauri which is 4.2 light years, or 25 trillion miles, away from us (There are 6 trillion miles in one light year, and the nearest galaxy to us is 132 billion light years away.) Though our brains can't take this in, it clearly means that we are not the center of, or of vital importance to, this vast unknowable cosmos. However if you are discouraged by that, I would remind you that all of us are still a small part of this immense, mysterious and amazing wonder. Some believe (and I am one of them) that everything in the cosmos is coming together to be more complex (like quarks to atoms, atoms to molecules, molecules to cells, and cells to brains). It is this great, cosmic, unifying, evolutionary process that allows us to think, reflect and be aware.

Why aren't we paying any attention to all of this? I don't really know but I think it's the same reason why we pay no attention to our increasing demise as a species. It's because we've become so caught up in ourselves with our myths of control and importance that we can't get out to see anything else...so we just don't care.

(I'll address this further when I talk about how science and cosmology can help us to understand The Way. If you want to know more about human evolution and extinction you can find them in Appendices II and V at the end of the book,

Clearly we are an evolved species that is one of the most complex animals on the planet Earth (of course there are many other complex animals). The cells in our bodies have come together so much in our evolution that with our incredibly complex computer-brains we are now able to reflect in upon ourselves, and out upon everything around us. Sure we a amazing, but we must never forget that we are mammals that have evolved to be unique in being able to think, reflect, and make choices. Our amazing reflective abilities do not make us any "better" than other animals, plants, or other life forms with whom we share the ecosystems of Earth. No, the complexity of our brains just allow us to understand more about ourselves and our surroundings than the other animals and plant. I think we are like the oldest child in a vast family who has been given more responsibility for taking care of the other children (plants and animals), as well as helping his mother (the Earth). Obviously we should be assisting, rather than using and abusing, the other life forms around us, and we should be helping our mother Earth to evolve rather than destroying her land, water, air and ecosystems. It's obvious to me that we have used the great reflective abilities that evolution has given us very poorly!

Why would we do such irresponsible, unethical things? Why have we chosen a path of selfish pride that tries to put ourselves and our species over everything else to divides us. It has left us overpopulating and polluting everything to kill off all life forms of the Earth, including ourselves! I've found that it's common knowledge that we will be extinct in between 200 to 1200 years. Scientists like Steven Hawking, David Attenborough, and Frank Fenner are adamant about this, and Fenner says it will come in just 100 years. This means that our species will have lived only 200 *thousand* of the Earth's 4 *billion* years (close to the 175 million years that the dinosaurs lived). The dinosaurs became extinct because of a meteor strike, whereas we are the ones systematically wiping-out the ecosystems to wipe out many of the Earth"s life forms including ourselves. Thus we, as a supposedly intelligent species, are committing suicide! Of course the Earth will reconstruct itself and go on, but we will not. There is no doubt that our prideful, greedy, blind actions are destroying our species...they are destroying us!

There is a large group, called the Human Extinction movement, which addresses the fact that we are a deviant, insane species ravaging the Earth. They say that we must stop our overpopulation right now and become a supporter of mother Earth and her life support ecosystems. A few go so far as to encourage us, as responsible reflective beings, to do away with our species to save the Earth. Of course I don't buy into this because I've always been aware of an underlying, good side of our species. At one time I associated this good side with what I called "God", but after my study of all the world's religions, I can't really do that anymore because I now find that concept to be an anthropomorphic, self-centered superstition.

So then, where *does* this good side of us originate? What is behind the fact that most of us have a conscience that attempts to tell us right from wrong, and the fact that we know love, honesty and compassion that helps us to work for justice, equality, and decency? For a while I couldn't answer this, so I drifted in confusion. However now I've seen and come to know where this deep longing for goodness, love and peace comes from. It comes from The Way of the cosmos that is in us, the cosmos and everything.

I also saw something else. I saw why as a reflective species we would do such idiotic things to ourselves, each other, and the other species of the Earth. I discovered a sick emotion in us that is is behind this insanity? In my last book I wrote how it has become accepted, and we've become so accustom to it, that we can't imagine anything else. .

I found that around 10 thousand years ago we began to embrace and even worship the deviant emotion that is called such things as *selfishness, pride, arrogance, greed or any number of other names.* (Remember, life evolved 4 *billion* years ago, Hominoids evolved just one *million* years ago, and Homo sapiens evolved only 200 *thousand* years ago. I've found that this separating and destructive selfish pride took over just 10 or 15 thousand years ago.) Pride has become such an obsession that we've built everything in our lives around it. It has not only been accepted, but we have become enslaved by it.

It's clear to me that self-centered arrogance, pride and greed have become our accepted norm. Individual-pride, group-pride, and species-pride, now rule us...and, to put it bluntly, they're taking us out! We are miserable in our *individual pride* (with its competition, fear, and anger); our *group pride* (as it builds antagonism between religions, nations, sexes, and races to create violence and massive wars). However even more dramatic is our colossal *species pride* that is wiping out the plants, animals, ecosystems as we evolve into extinction. Obviously we haven't just taken a wrong turn; we've become totally lost! We took the wrong road of divisive pride to ignore the connecting force of The Way. (We'll talk more in detail about all of this later.)

Recently we have begun to see that we are not a special, ordained, or even very bright species. We've also seen that we're not the only reflective species in the cosmos. because we now know there are millions or billions of others out there. We have also *not* been put on the Earth to rule over it or anything, because we are only one of many species that are interconnected to each other and everything else. In fact the whole cosmos is a vast, interconnected web. We see can see that everywhere in the evolution of the cosmos, in the evolution of life on the Earth, and even in our own personal evolution each day. We are always evolving and changing as we get older to grow in our education and understanding, as we grow in our emotions and relationships, as our finances fluctuate and change, and on and on. Everything in this great interconnected web we call the cosmos is evolving.

In our interconnected state, we should have long ago seen our connection to the Earth's life-support systems we call *"ecosystems"*. We should have been made aware of this early on in our evolution because the ecosystems are so vitally important to our survival. In this complex system, each life-form is interconnected to all of the others . What happens to one happens to all, and nature's balancing of the ecosystems is what sustains life and keeps it going on the Earth. However because of our species self-centered pride and greed with its worship of accumulated wealth, we've lost our way to ignore and cast out this obvious reality. Instead we're holding on to arrogant, superstitious of ourselves which are acted out in our treatment of this planet. We are casually wiping out the Earth's life-forms through our overpopulation, pollution, and the murder of plants and animals. *(I would urge you again to read Appendices V.)*

I realize that this is not pleasant, but from where I stand, it's the only picture of us that is true. Of course we could change, but do we have enough time? Up until recently The Way, that is in us all, has been moving us together, so that even in our state of pride, we have progressively made some moral advances. However recently industrialization's pollution (beginning around 1760) and overpopulation's fueling of animal slaughter and deforestation, have so destroyed the delicate balance of the ecosystems that we now face extinction. This towers over my life, and it should (and must soon) tower over everybody's life. If we can stop covering-up and escaping these realities and wake-up, perhaps it is still possible to change. However this can only happen if we can regain The Way as our guide and motivation. That's why I'm writing this book... because right now as intelligent, reflective beings we do have the opportunity and power to change through recognizing and following what I call The Way. *(If you are interested in reading a more detailed study of Human evolution, I have recorded some of my research on this subject in Appendices II at the back of the book.)*

The Way is infinite, eternal.
Why is it eternal?
It was never born;
thus it can never die.
Why is it infinite?
It has no desire for itself;
thus it is present for all beings. Tao te Ching

II. A Look at The Way?

1.

I will now offer you a look at what I mean by The Way, so you can see where this book is going. The Way has been ignored but it is not lost. No, it's just that few right now recognize it, so it can't be identified or discussed. There are clear indications that our ancient ancestors knew about The Way, but in the face of our recent *de*volution into self-centered arrogance, it has vanished...but is still right there!

The Way is in everything, so we should see it in many places, things, writings and our-self. Also this is not the first time it has been named The Way. In this book you will see how this title keeps popping up to describe wise teachings and movements that reflect its presence. So this is not a new idea, or even a new name for it, since it has existed since the evolution of the cosmos began.

As I've said, my realization of this truth came to me gradually from my research, but it has also come out of my own life's evolution...as will also be true for you. Thus I now see that this concept has always been inside of me and

it's clear to me now that it is absolutely necessary for reflective beings to survive. We shouldn't say we have *lost* The Way; we should say that we have covered it over with selfishness, pride and greed to desert it. However The Way is still within us waiting to be released.

I believe that what's left of The Way in us is what keeps us from abusing, stealing, murdering, etc.. It is the voice of what we call "conscience" and the force we know as love. It should be easy to describe, but it's not at all. I've found that The Way stretches my limited abilities to describe it with only my measly words. It, like the cosmos with its evolution, will always remain a mystery that we'll never pin down. However we can still know that the cosmos and The Way are there...that they both exist. Therefore even now we can still be open to allow The Way with its mystical powers to arise and guide us. We can enter into its power at any time to live and have a future.

The Way is something that reflective beings should instinctively know and embrace, but it's more than that. The Way is more than just the moral foundation at the base of the cosmos' that is bringing all things together in complexity, and which we (and all reflective beings) must choose to bring us together. It's more than the only course humans can take to continue to be a meaningful, lasting part of the Earth and the cosmos. It's also much more than another of our humanly evolved traditions that comes from our superstitions (religious or otherwise), our dress codes, our menus, our social orders and practices, or our educational and family practices. It's outside of all humanly contrived things, and when we become a part of it, it puts most of these traditions in their place as silly, passing, habits coming out of our pride. In fact The Way is more than we can ever comprehend because it's present in everything in the cosmos and is totally beyond our control.

2.

The Way can be seen in the order, interconnection, and oneness of the cosmos. When we perceive this, we use human words such as "the laws of nature" or "the laws of science" or "scientific principals" or even "evolution". We see it in the animals who (by instinct) bond with a mate and live in a group to tenderly care for and protect their young. (If you say these actions are *just* instinct, then I would ask, what brings about instincts?) :I believe it's something that is even deeper and more profound than gravity (in matter) as it brings all of cosmic evolution together to be more than it was before.

All I'm trying to say is that nature, science and the cosmos have an order to them that allows evolution to advance, but it can't be pined down. Over time many have pretended to know what it is and even thought they could control it. They've said that it comes from a human-like father or mother figure up in the sky that we can talk to and get stuff. This comfortable, very easy explanation has been called by such names as God, Allah, Yahweh, or hundreds of others. Also various superstitions like spirits who do amazing things have been identified with this. Great stories and myths have evolved around all of these things over the years that continue to grow. And then of course there are some who've just ignored the existence of science and the laws of nature.

I have sympathy for those who've said that we just have no idea what began, or is behind, the order we can see in the cosmos, because we know so little about the cosmos. Also as a freshly evolved reflective species that has only recently identified that there is cosmic order, our ignorance is not surprising. It's always silly when we don't admit our limitations, but on this one I have to say that though we can't fully understand this order, we are still aware that it is there.

Thus I believe that the reason that the laws and principals of nature exist is because of an ordering, moral ethic that lies at the base of the cosmos, which I call The Way. I believe that it's in things like the *Four Forces of the cosmos* that consist of:

1. The *Strong Force* that holds atoms together,
2. The *Weak Force* that is behind radioactive decay and neutrinos,
3. The *Electra-magnetic Force* that is behind electricity and magnetism,
4. *The Gravitational Force* that acts on matter.
   (Some say that the fifth force is *Time,* but others believe that time is something   called *Modified Gravity.*)

I believe that the The Way is associated with all of these things, as well as all of the order and reason we see. We see it in both science, ethics, and the moral tugs we feel in our reflective lives ((like our conscience, sense of justice, sympathy, and peace). All I've done in this book is to give this cosmic ordering force a name.

I also believe we can see The Way in our own lives in words that pull us together such as *"humility, love, unity, compassion"* and many others that we'll discuss later. As I said, all of these things pull us together as reflective beings, so all of these words thus lead us to The Way. I believe that for reflective beings The Way might be called "the law of a meaningful, sustainable life". (If you find the term "law" offensive, just remember the many references to laws in things like the laws of science, the law of Hammurabi from ancient Babylon, the Ten Commandments from Moses, or the Sermon on The Mount ("A new commandment I give you") from Jesus, and a hosts of others. I believe that The Way is, as many religious leaders who have taught, "written on our hearts". I believe it's a basic, necessary part of who we are that we've ignored to leave ourselves in big, big trouble.

3.

The Way is natural to us because it's still in us, but as reflective beings, who are uniquely capable of choosing for ourselves, we have chosen *not* to follow it. I think it's a bit like eating or breathing, where we can choose not to do them, but if we do, we die. The urge to follow The Way is just as much there and important as eating or breathing, but our species has insanely decided to choose pride over The Way...and our species (dragging other species with it) will soon die out.

The Way is not something that we can casually talk about or visualize. It's not a thing, a place, or a destination, and it's also not something to find since it's always been there and always will be. It's not even something we can teach, talk about, or even do, because it's actually who we already are. When we enter The Way, we become The Way and we come home. All we need to do is accept it, step into it, and with each of our evolutions, move together and advance into the cosmos as reflective beings enjoying a future.

I think The Way could be said to be a little bit like a direction. Perhaps it could be said to be the direction of the cosmos and all of conscious evolution. I believe it's clearly the direction of all sustainable, reflective life-forms that we must take if we are to survive. It could be said to be like the East or West, or North or South, where if you choose the wrong one, you're lost. There are many directions we can take in life, but most of the time we just follow the one right in front of us that we're used to and have become accustom to...and right now that one is self-centered pride that disconnects.

If we ever do think about where we're going, it's usually about reaching a financial goal, getting a better job, being patriotic, getting into heaven, or of course pleasing everybody. All of these things are self-centered, shallow, immediate goals that leave out the existence of other people, other cultures, other species, and certainly the Earth and the cosmos. They leave out everything but me, me, me! And of course when *everybody* is just for me, me, me, the results are disastrous – like what we have today. Face it, we live in a chaotic mess where nobody's really happy and within a species that's going out because of its greedy abuse of the Earth. The Way for us should be a cherished map emblazoned on our hearts that is leading us toward a meaningful life and a real future.

The Way brings all mater and consciousness in the cosmos together to be ever more complex. Thus as a part of the cosmos we must follow The Way to come together with each other and other species to evolve and survive within the Earth's interconnected ecosystems. We should have evolved to understand our interconnection to everything and most especially each other, but we have not. In our pride, we think we are all that matters, so we pay no attention to other people. Pride has caused us to be sociopaths in the ways we treat each other. (Psychopaths are people who have no conscience at all so you can find them mostly in prisons, whereas sociopaths are those who have lost almost all of their conscience...like us.) Since we've become locked within ourselves, we can't see out. We don't recognize and appreciate the wonder, likeness and pain of other people, so we just treat them like dirt. However The Way is compassion, love, truth and real. It's the direction that all reflective beings in the cosmos must choose if they are to exist.

The Way is also ancient, progressive, mystical, and incredibly wise, so as you can see, it's trivial to sum it up in limited, human words. However I've found that I can better understand and communicate The Way by observing what I've perceived to be *"word-paths"* that bring us together and lead us to The Way. Some of these word-paths might be communicated in such words as: "**humility, love, compassion, kindness, peace, justice, forgiveness, sympathy, empathy, giving, equality, egalitarianism, freedom, oneness, unity, intimacy, honesty and democracy**". However there are multiple other words that bring us together and might be called paths to The Way, but the words I've mentioned here have helped me to envision and approach the wonders of The Way, so I'm passing them on. Still please remember that The Way itself will always remain outside the realm of any of our words or thoughts.

It can only be understood if we can get out of ourselves to find our own unique path to The Way. Through these words, I'm trying to share with you my mental picture of the unnameable force that is pulling us together. The scientific law of gravity is about pulling matter together, but matter is not all there is to the cosmos, so we have to ask what is behind all the things (like consciousness or awareness) that are also being pulled together? This cosmic force remains one of the many things about the cosmos that remains a mystery. All we can know now is that this unifying force that I have named The Way, is attempting to guide us, and everything else in the cosmos, together, and that it is necessary that all reflective life-forms in the cosmos chose it so they can continue to evolve.

Though these word-paths can only help us to paint a mental picture of The Way, all of these word-paths are important within themselves. Still we must remember that brushes, canvases and colors are not the painting. The Way exists on it own and will always be more than any of our mental pictures. The Way is natural and all-inclusive, so it is found in world religions, ethics, poetry, prose, plays, and is even in the motivational ethics of caring doctors, police, politicians, social workers, and maybe super-heroes. If we were in The Way, we would know the security, peace, unity and real community we now so long for.

Pride wipes out our ability to see the obvious. As a species, we should be able to see that separating ourselves from and destroying the Earth's ecosystems is ridiculous! We should also be able to see The Way as the underlying force of who we really are and what can make us authentic and real. We should be able to make it our major goal in life!

4.

The concept of The Way (and my urge to write about it) came to me when I saw that the same ethic or morality is found in all of the world's religions. I also recognized The Way's presence in philosophy. psychology, ethics and my reading of pros and poetry. I was fascinated when I saw that it's clearly the thing that is bringing all of the different religions together because The Way is the opposite of the pride, greed, selfishness that tears them apart. Obviously The Way is not tied to the exclusive superstitions and bureaucratic power mongers that keep religions fighting with each other.

In religions, The Way is a part of the Ten Commandments. It's what Jesus, Mohammad, Buddha,

Lao-tzu, Confucius, the eleven gurus of Sikhism, and the founders of almost all other religions taught. It's also a large part of what Humanists have taught down through the ages. It's found in classrooms that teach philosophy, ethics, poetry, and prose. Even though we ignore it in our worship of pride and superstitions, The Way still remains a part of who we are. In fact I believe that it's what's holding together the torn, abused relationships that we have left. If The Way in religion and other things was accepted as the underlying ethic of our reflective species, we would be unified, at peace and vastly different.

Though this cosmic ethic is a fundamental part of every religion and is often preached by followers of their religion's early teachings, it is seldom followed. I have witnessed a constant struggle that is going on in the different religions between things that reflect the unity and peace of The Way, and things that encourage the separating, exclusive, pride-filled, superior judgmental-ism that is tearing them apart.

However, the fact is that The Way is still at the base of most religions, and this fact is one of the main things that helped me to write of this book. I saw a place where the world's religions moved past their exclusive pride enough to actually get together! When they did so, they've agreed on the basic precepts that point to what I have come to call The Way. I also saw that when they've actually managed to follow these precepts and work together, it has come from their unknowing affirmation of The Way.

Most people are shocked to find that the world's religions are even talking, much less coming together, because their fighting and disagreements are all that's ever reported. However, the first **Parliament of World Religions** met on September 11, 1893 in Chicago with representatives from most of the world's religions. It was followed later by others in 1993, 1999, 2004, 2007, 2009, 2004 and 2015. In studying these gatherings, it's become clear to me that the mindset of the participants, as well the joint affirmations they made, were clear manifestations of The Way. I've seen that if the religions of the world are to further respect each other and work together, it will come out of their mutual respect for The Way that is in them. Let me say again that when I studied these gatherings, I found that unifying pull of The Way was the underlying subject and inspiration of the parliament's gatherings and was found in all of their agreements.

Also when I was reading about and researching how the world religions came together to make up these parliaments, it suddenly hit me that these values and morals that they agreed upon were motivating them to come together and should be bringing our species together! I realized that if we had chosen to follow these agreements, we would have moved together in the same way that matter and energy in the cosmos are moving together!

I saw that we should have naturally come together as a species, but we have not...and I saw why! It's because we as a reflective species have chosen to reject it, and replace it with a divisive, separating emotion that has many names, but I call it pride. Making all of these connections was an *"Ah-ha"* moment of awareness that I shall never forget.

I was very excited, because for the first time concerning what's going in us, I had an explanation that makes real sense...and I also had a natural, rational way that me might be able to halt our present falling state. It meant there can be some hope for our future, but this can only happen if we can find, see and claim the power of The Way.

(To read further about the Parliaments of World Religions, you can look at Appendices I at the conclusion of this book.)

The supreme good is like water,
which nourishes all things without trying to.
It is content with the low places that people distain
Thus it is like The Way.
So In dwelling, live close to the ground,
In thinking, keep to the simple,
In conflict, be fair and generous,
In governing, don't try to control,
In work, do what you enjoy'
In family life, be completely present.

Tao te Ching

III. Blocks to The Way

My goal in writing this is to allow you to see The Way. There are many reasons why we turn a blind eye toward obvious truths, but let me mention some reasons why I think we discount and ignore "The Way". Unless we can recognize and deal with these blocks, I don't see how we'll ever be able to really approach The Way.

Pride and Greed

(We've talked a little about Pride and greed before, but they are so important and serious that they deserve more individual attention. They are are almost the same and are the biggest enemy of The Way.)

Pride

In the earlier book that I referred to called <u>The Absurdity of Pride and the Peace of Humility,</u> I talked about how pride (with its arrogance, greed and hypocrisy) is a deviant evolution that is destroying our ability to live joyful, peaceful lives. I also pointed out how, pride as a species, it's leading us into extinction. This book has chapters on *individual pride* (that destroy our relationships in marriage, work, and friendships), on *group pride* (that is destroying the relationships of nations, religions, and social and cultural groupings such as race, sex, work, wealth, education and others). It also talked about *species pride* (that causes us to feel superior to the other species and casually destroy them, as well as much of the Earth itself). This book talks about how pride has ushered in this disconnecting and abusive evolution, but it also offers us things we can do to *release ourselves* from the scourge of pride. I would urge you to read it because it is crucial that we learn about pride and what it's doing to us so we can turn away from it to enter The Way.

Pride is clearly a deviant emotion that tears us apart, yet we have allowed it, like a cancer, to spread into our minds and lives. The parallels between cancer in our bodies, and pride in our minds, is a very serious one. Cancer is an uncontrollable growth of cells that grow into tumors in the body that spreads into other areas through our lymphatic systems and our blood. Pride is the uncontrollable growth of a disconnecting, sick emotion that has spread into other emotions to alter the functioning of our minds. It effects every aspect of our lives to destroy us in our individual relationships, our group relationships and our species relationships. If cancer is not stopped by treatment, it can lead to death. If pride is not stopped by the common sense wisdom of The Way, it will lead us into massive divisions that lead to violence, war, and ultimately the death of our species.

As I mentioned above I break pride into the three groups of *individual pride, group pride* and *species pride*. Of these, I believe that *group pride* is most misunderstood. People often join groups to have some community or to feel a part of something bigger than themselves...and there's nothing wrong with that. However because we are mired in pride, most of the groups we join are prideful, exclusive, and mean-spirited. We often join them to feel accepted, popular or even superior to others without any further thought about them. However even though most groups are like that, not all of them are. I'm just saying that we need to reflect on the make-up and purpose of any group we decide to join to see whether it's based on pride or The Way. I confess that because of this problem, I now belong to very few groups, and I'm sometimes called a recluse because I find most groups around me to be distasteful. Each of us needs to seriously reflect on the groups we're considering...and be very careful. It's much harder to get out of a group after you've gotten entangled, than it is to turn it down before you join.

Thus this complex emotional thing we call pride is now touted everywhere as wonderful, when actually it is terrible! Pride is so divisive and lethal that nothing about it is good. Thus I believe that there is no question that recognizing and fighting pride is the greatest issue of our day and is necessary to finding The Way. However it's not being addressed at all because it's become a major part of who we are. When we are a able to see what it's doing to us, we will be able to regain our ability to discuss humility (the condition where pride is not), and maybe even grow to be humble enough to come together rather than fall apart. Also then it's not hard to see our crying need to reclaim the lost wonder of unconditional love, which like humility, is the opposite of pride and leads to The Way.

Greed

Remember pride and greed are the same thing. That's because greed is pride applied to money, our possessions or other tangible things. Greed is certainly found in the stuff we accumulate, but *most of the time it refers to money*. It has spread all over the world, and like pride has wiped out our reflective abilities to take us over. Today money is no more seen as an exchange that helps us to survive, but as something we n must have more and more. It's addictive in that the more we have, the more we want. We never get enough, and we lose sight of everything else.

It's also true in our present worldwide money system in that the more money we have, the more money we're able to get. What this means is that more and more people have more and more money, so less and less people have enough money to survive as starvation and poverty grow and grow. It's a really a disgusting mess. The shocking greed that this form of exchange has inspired has left only a very small percentage of the population with most of the money. These money addicts within our atrocious money distribution system also have most of the power (because money has become power), so these few continue to rule over and destroy the many. They even pay to stop anything from being done to end this disgraceful inequity. Any compassionate suggestions to change it is killed by the fact that everyone (even the poor) prop-up, admire and support the super-wealthy people who then ignore them. Any people who evolved out of their prideful, greedy money addiction are accused of being stupid, dangerous and even a traitor to their country. Money has evolved so far into greed that its abusive use is now accepted not only as normal but as heroic. Thus the world will no doubt remain stuck in this greedy, unjust, insane system of dispersing money until we go extinct.

Let me add that this is complicated by a debate about whether there should be big or small governments. Big, greedy businesses wants to throw off all over-sight and control from the government (which is all there is to stop the rich from doing whatever they want and unethically make as much money as they can). Thus they constantly lobby saying that government itself is bad (especially in regard to taxes), so governments need to be limited and very small. Some say that government is dangerous and taking over our lives. They also lobby saying that governments hurt the poor and are their enemy. The sad thing is that a lot of poor people believe this nonsense. They even elect the very rich to office and make heroes out of them. Of course not all rich people are so sunk in greed that they are blind to the problems of the poor, but I've found money-greed to be so powerful that it's very hard for for a rich person not to be addicted and totally out of touch with The Way.

I continue to find it strange that poor people blindly trust big business to be moral and flawless so they need no policing, while on the other hand they demand more police in the communities in which they live. Do they believe that only the individuals around them can be greedy and unethical...but large businesses can't? Hasn't it been proven over and over that both need to have some control? Of course, with our population growing from 1 billion to 7 billion in just the last century, greed is even more prevalent so the need for policing and protection in all areas grows every day. As the populations rises and we've become more overwhelmed, governments that are far too small leave greedy, unethical behavior untouched. Of course the greedy rich and powerful who make money out of divisive competition, military build-up, war, and the rape of the Earth try to convince us that all of this is good and beneficial, while they show no concern for the poor that make up most of the world. I think this is not only unethical; it's evil!

Let me mention something further. Greed is a huge player in our move to extinction. Greed and money made from ignoring the environment are making it impossible to even discuss changes that could avoid our pollution of the land, water and air. That's because such reforms might require big business to diminish some of their millions and billions of profits. For them, losing even a little money is unthinkable. Our pollution is ridiculous, however the greed of big money continues to lobby those in power to keep us all ignorant about what we're doing to the Earth and its ecosystems. They are determined to halt any attempt to change anything. Corporate pride and greed have got to go! This greed is one of the biggest blocks to our future and is a total block to The Way.

Another dimension of Pride and Greed

a. Why?

How have we've allowed pride and greed to take us over like this? *Why* have we chosen pride and greed and allowed it to destroy our natural, unifying humility and peace. For some time now I've known that pride and greed are behind most of the misery of our species and is leaving us divided, fighting and falling into extinction. However *I did not know **why** as an intelligent species we would choose such* *a horrible thing as pride. I did not know what had allowed this total disaster to happen.*

Now I know it's because we discarded and drifted away apart from The Way. We've evolved so far away from it that our culture, values, and lives are now wrapped up in pride's nonsense. *Without the guidance of The Way* we've thrown away our natural humility and welcomed in an unnatural, demented emotion of pride. Let me say again that there is no possible way we could do such a stupid, tragic, lethal thing if we were in touch with The Way. Thus the truth is that in losing The Way, we've lost our mind! Any sense of The Way would have identified this dangerous, destructive emotion that I call pride/greed and allowed us to eliminated it. That's because pride/greed is not only different from The Way; it could be said to be its exact opposite!

Do we still have a chance to stop this foolishness? Can we throw off pride to regain our natural humility (and decency) to have a lasting place in the cosmos? Can we still evolve into The Way? These are towering questions because it would mean that we would have to reverse our present course and put ourselves in tune with this core ethic of cosmos and be real. Of course pride is aware that The Way is its nemesis, so pride that reigns within us will fight and discredit The Way to the end. Obviously it won't be easy.

However, there is still some good news: The Way that is made up of humility, love and peace is much more powerful than any of the silly nonsense of disconnecting pride. Thus I believe The Way can ultimately prevail. Of course the bad news is that it may not prevail within our species, but it definitely will prevail throughout the cosmos in other reflective species who are able to evolve into The Way. From that we can take some comfort...but not so much that we can stop fighting the pride and greed that is in us and in our world right now. We are Homo sapiens and we must do all that we can to stop pride's insane influence and destruction of each one of us and our species. We must also do all that we can to save our fellow, other species from any further extinction. (We have been so cruel to them that for me it's agony to even think about.) The only way that anything will be done is if we find and enter in The Way, and that must be done quickly.

b. Two Ethics

I've only recently found another shocking truth that has been lying mute within me but has now jumped out to shock me. There is no doubt that because our species has lived in pride and greed for so long, pride has taken us over to become our ethic. (Ethics are moral principles that govern conduct or behavior.) However since I've seen and studied The Way, I find myself face to face with *another ethic,* and this ethic is real, sustainable and actually makes sense.. Thus I must conclude that there are (and of course have been) *two different ethical principles* within and around us all the time that I call pride/greed and The Way...and right now the wrong one is winning.

For instance the ethic of selfishness, greed, money, militancy, war, nationalism, building boarders, hate of differences, prejudice, meanness, ignoring suffering, etc., rules the day. This ethic is now the driving force of our lives so it is never questioned.

On the other hand there is another ethic out there of uniting love that's calling us to compassion, giving, finding peace, accepting differences, seeing humanity as one, entering into suffering, always seeking oneness, and many others. This is the ethic that pulls us together to live in love, peace and community, Though this ethic still exists within us (which sometimes comes out in our religions, intelligence and interactions with others), this ethic is being ignored, not followed, and rejected.

So we have two ethics, but one of them is winning even though deep down we know it's wrong, and the other is still there but is called idealistic, impractical and naive. The one that makes sense is cast out to leave us in our misery with a nonexistent future. Two ethics, and everyday we are choosing the one that's tearing us apart as we follow whatever our parents teach us or where mindless others lead.

Somehow we have to wake up. We must recognize these two ethics within us (by first discovering the second one called The Way), and then we must courageously step out for ourselves and choose between them.. We must use our reflective abilities (perhaps for the first time) to see, be real, and actually care.

After that we must move on to *change our angry, judging, exclusive culture* (culture is defined as collective human manifestations and achievements). The ethic of pride/greed has created this culture, so we must work to create a new culture of humility, love, caring and peace that propels us into a life lived long and well. Thus we have two ethics with two cultures, but only one of them both makes sense that can bring us happiness and allow us to survive. The choice of The Way is there...but will we take it...can we take it?

(If you're interested in my opinion on some details of what following the ethic of The Way might involve, you can turn to the last chapter of the book.)

Escapes from Reality

I have said that we have evolved into an escapist culture that's trying to cover up our problems, and in the process, we've covered up The Way. For some people today, everything they do is an escape, and for the rest, most of what what they do is escape. This is because we are motivated by something that drives us into a meaningless, violent life that is so ridiculous that we need to escape from it. Escape is who we've become, It's who we are. This may sound strange, but if you think about it, you can see that it's true.

Thus we have a swarm of good reasons to escape, because the horrible results of our pride are festering within us. For instance, our *individual pride* destroys our personal relationships (that leaves us fighting, separated and alone); our *group pride* destroys our national, religious, racial and other relationships (that leaves us threatened, frightened, and surrounded by violence and war); and our *species pride* destroys our relationship with the Earth and its many life-forms (that leaves us living in a grossly overpopulated, polluted, unhealthy world where we're going extinct). That is certainly enough to justify trying to escape! I have to admit that some small escapes might even be necessary just to keep us sane, however we overdo them. We erase our minds and our hearts to a point where we're unable to think or do anything about this monstrous mess.

Because of all of this, it seems overwhelming to approach this subject, so I'll try to break it down into three manageable groups. I'll call the first group is "Not So Bad Escapes", the second group is

"Moderately Bad Escapes", and the last one is "Really Bad Escapes". There are many escapes that are not so bad if taken in small doses but terrible if used a lot. This means that many of our escapes are not only over-done, but they've become addictive...or too much of anything can be harmful.

All of our escapes are bad because they limit our ability to see and reflect. They all keep us from being who we are...from being real and facing the truth...from acting sensibly...from properly evolving into the cosmos to be a viable contributing part of it's evolution. They are so ingrained in us that we take them for granted. Thus I'm attempting a very unpleasant and probably impossible task here, so be patient.

Obviously too much alcohol is the first thing that comes to mind when you talk about escapes and it is a big one, but I could also mention things like illegal over-the-counter or prescribed drugs, television, work, sports, recreation, sitting down too much, shopping too much, sleeping too much, having sex too much, using computers and i-phones too much, doing exciting or dangerous things too much, and other things. Most of our lives are spent in escapes because most of our lives are spent in fear, frustration, loneliness, confusion and misery.

Not So Bad Escapes

a. One example of this is too much *exercise* . It's wonderful to get enough of it to circulate and clean out our blood, our bodies and our minds. It is commonly accepted that exercise is good. However we may become obsessed with it and use it as an escape from everything, and that is bad.

b. Also it looks like we can become equally obsessed with to much *recreation* which makes us use it as a way of escape. Some recreation is obviously good, but when our lives start being built around it, it can detract us from us looking at what's real.

c. The same thing can be said of *sleep*. Many people use sleep to escape from reality rather than as the healthy endeavor we do at night. We can sleep too much to find ourselves sleeping-in and not getting up, or we can sleep too little, which is just dangerous.

d. *Adventurous endeavors* can be dangerous and can also be an escape. They can give a gigantic Adrenalin rush that can become addictive. I have known people who have throw away their lives in some dangerous, escapist, adrenaline pursuit.

e. *Sitting down* may seem like a silly thing to mention, but when we do it all the time, reports say that it can be bad. I hesitated to mention this because it doesn't seem like an escape...but maybe it is. It is clear that our bodies are not made for extensive sitting, because only a short time ago in our evolution, people were standing all the time and would only stop standing to sleep. Now much of the work-force, as well as retired people, are sitting all the time...and it doesn't take a genius to know that's not good.

Moderately Bad Escapes

a. Movies or radio can be a problem, but of course *television* is the biggest problem and is one of our major escapes. For some of us, television takes up the major part of our day, so we become lost in it. It becomes our friend, companion and even our family. I am fully aware that if television is used in a selective and educational way, it can be very helpful, but when it takes over our lives in watching shallow comedy and drama, it is just an huge escape.

b. Associated somewhat with television is *sports* because before we had television, our ability to watch sports was vastly limited. To occasionally play a sport for recreation is certainly not bad, but to become obsessed with either playing or watching to the point where we think of little else, is bad. We all know that watching sports on television has become "the national pastime". The most watched sport in the world is soccer, however baseball, rugby, football, basketball, golf, tennis, cricket, but cars and dogs and horses racing (which is another abuse of animals), and boxing (which abuses people) are also right up there. In the United States, football has become a big, big business, and it uses up vast amounts of money, time, and people's lives. All of this can clog our minds with competitive, inconsequential trivia, and in some cases it can even cause players in violent sports to have concussions. Sports has certainly become a huge escape.

c. I-phones and computers have also become a major source of escape. They take people over o use vast amounts of time. I have increasingly seen children and young adults who are so addicted to them that they can't seem to think about anything else. I heard recently that the sidewalks of many cities have become dangerous because people walk blindly forward with their eyes buried in their i-phones.

d. *Work* is obviously necessary for most of us, but when work becomes all we think about, it can be an escape. Actually doing too much work can ruin our relationships, severely limit our interests, and threaten the health of our bodies and minds. I have known people who have been so absorbed in their work that they've escaped from everything else.

e. *Shopping* is also a part of who we've evolved to be, but when it's overdone, it becomes a terrible escape. It can put people into bankruptcy, destroy their marriages, and bring about deep depression and grief. This is not an uncommon thing, but it's usually covered up so we don't hear about it...and that's sad, because it can be addressed and dealt with through counseling.

f. *Sex* is our natural response to a certain gender, and when it's controlled, it can be very nice. However when it is not controlled and allowed to take us over, it can be a very sick escape! It can not only destroy the person involved, but it can destroy other people around them. I have seen people's lives maimed by broken promises, abuse and rape. Rape is a horrible form of assault, and it is much more common than we think. It takes place too many times in too many places! Only recently have we started talking about sexual obsessions and sexual addictions. It is now seen as an addiction like alcoholism, and we're beginning to set up rehabilitation centers to address it. But the point is that sex, like so many other things, can take us over to become an unfortunate, dangerous escape from reality that robs us of who we really are.

Really Bad Escapes

a. Drinking *Alcohol* can be disastrous if we aren't careful and are physically and psychologically prone to alcoholism. Also many of us become what's called "a problem drinker", where we over-use alcohol to a point where it limits our other activities. Drinking too much alcohol can alienate us from the people around us and even threaten our lives and even the lives of others. Still some doctors say that one or two drinks at the end of the day may actually be helpful. It can help us with stress as it offers us some relaxation. However all doctors agree drinking can be dangerous, and that is seen in the shocking statistics of its abuse all over the world. For that reason, I would conclude that we should put alcohol in the Really Bad category even if we are able to take it in moderation because it can end up ruining lives.

b. This same thing can be said for over-the-counter, *prescribed or illegal drugs*. Legal drugs do a lot of good when they are taken responsibly to assist our health, but when they're abused, they become disastrous. Such abuse has actually been on the rise in recent years as people try to use the various results of the poppy (like cocaine) to escape their pain and depression. The USA has spent billions of dollars trying to stop the traffic of illegal drugs to no avail. That's because the truth is that the growing and delivery of drugs can't be stopped (just as alcohol couldn't be stopped in prohibition). The heroin epidemic all over the world is wiping people out every day, and nobody can found a way to stop it. I am actually for legalizing some drugs because prosecuting less serious drugs like marijuana (which is not as dangerous as cigarettes) just ends up destroying young lives by putting them into jail, and also wasting vast resources to keep them thee that are needed elsewhere. I believe that the only thing that can really help to stop poppy drugs from being used (and can be done with much smaller amount of the expenditure) is to educate the public (especially children in the schools) on the huge problems associated with taking these drugs. We must stop putting people in jail because taking drugs in excess should not be see as a crime *but as an addiction. T*hose who are hooked on drugs are sick. They need help and need to treated as we treat every other disease.

They find themselves living a tragic life that needs our compassion and our help.

c. Another real concern is our *escape from the sufferings of others* as we pretend that suffering don't exist in the world. This often comes out of our class pride, but it can also come from national, racial, or economic pride. Escaping from the sufferings of others is behind things like world illiteracy, poverty, disease, and even war (where millions of innocent people are killed, turned into refugees, and forgotten). This escape also encourages stereotyping, prejudice and fear that leaves us unjust and mean. When we escape from other people's suffering and pretend that it doesn't exist, it makes us deaf and blind to reality. Just because we have been given the opportunity to live a plentiful life with food, water, medical care, housing, and a pleasant, violent free neighborhood certainly doesn't mean that everybody has it. That's what escape does; it makes us think that somehow we deserve (or have earned) all these things. It also makes us conclude that those who don't have what we have must be dumb, lazy, irresponsible, or even dangerous. We exercise this prejudice by separating ourselves from those who are suffering by living in gated communities or exclusive developments that do all they can to keep "unacceptable" people out. It's obvious that this form of escape makes people mean, unfeeling and even, at times, dangerous. I have said that class pride is one of the worst of the group prides because it makes us blind to suffering and pushes us to deny that we are connected to *everyone* on this planet...and as it does this, it dramatically blocks our access to The Way.

e. Another powerful thing that keeps us from facing the reality around us, is our escape into various *superstitions*. Of course our religions are full of them, but let me say again that I am not against the world's religion's early ethical and moral teachings. I am against the prideful superstitions that have evolved into them that make their adherents blessed and superior that draws them away from responsible actions toward other people, other species, and the Earth. I'm against anything that denies that we are a part of the Earth and the cosmos. We are not, as pride teaches, just responsible to *"me"*, worshiping something like *"me"*, that has chosen *"me"*, and will keep *"me"* safe. We are not just a part of *my* nationality, race, class or sex, because we're a part of everything, everywhere. When we blindly loose sight of that fact, we leave reality to block out The Way. For this reason, I have reservations about worshiping anything. When we worship something like a divine being, the Earth, some animal, a spirit, or some person (like a king or ruler, or hero)...when we worship anything, we divert ourselves away from real spiritual things like the experience of life everyday, the wonder of our ability to reflect, the miracle of the evolution of life, and being a part of the Earth and the cosmos. Superstitions are an attempt to make things simple or controllable as we escape reality. We try to solve all of our problems by putting our trust in something other than the natural evolution of the cosmos of which we're a part, and that is real. Thus if I were to worship anything, it might be the earth or the cosmos, because I know that they are there and that they are really that from which we have come. They are where we have come from, sustained us, and now offer us a future. All I'm saying is that the diversion from reality that comes out of superstitions in self-centered myths is one monster escape. They tell us that we don't need to worry about anything including our extinction because we are especially blessed and something out there (some higher being) is in charge who will solve everything for us. I think that this is one of the the biggest escapes that we face, and may also be one of the biggest blocks to The Way.

e. This one is happening everywhere and is controversial, and it's definitely the most covered up. It's called *suicide*. People commit suicide when they feel they have to escape from the mental or physical pain in their lives. It is certainly the most tragic escape when we see that it ignores and destroys our amazing senses, brains, complex bodies and everything. World wide statistics on it are hard to find, but in the U.S, it's the 10th leading cause of death at 42,773 suicides each year, and for every successful suicide there are 25 attempts that don't succeed. There are 22 veteran suicides each day, and the military reported that 265 active service-members committed suicide last year. (I believe that killing anything is repulsive to our reflective minds, yet we keep on killing all the time to become depressed and suicidal.) Suicide is now a raging epidemic that nobody addresses because it's so unthinkable. There is no question that this is the worst and most regretful of all escapes...what more can you say?

f. Another of the most serious and devastating escapes from reality that we face is our worldwide *national pride* that says that my nation is the best and really the only nation that exists. This pushes every country into thinking that it must defend itself to be protected from all these other "terrible people" who are not just like us. This spawns every nation to arm itself leading to a vast drain of resources in a arm's race. It develops a militaristic cultural (or "bubble" which I'll talk about later) that ultimately leads the nations into war. This militaristic mindset of any culture takes us over to make us not only insensitive to killing other people, but encourages us to do so...and teaches us how to do it. Some people in a nationalistic fervor, totally immerse themselves in this killing culture to loose sight of reality, and to escape and lose The Way.

We could discuss a bunch of other things that are escapes from reality, but I hope you get the point – any escape can block out reality and The Way. Also let me say again that a little bit of an escape may not be so bad and even understandable, but when it's taken too seriously (especially when we become immersed and dependent on it), it becomes dangerous. However all escapes to some extent prevent us from seeing or doing anything about the real problems that need our immediate attention. They prevent us from seeing the truth of our nonsensical ways so we never do anything. Such escapes rob our ability to perceive The Way, because The Way rests on the truth and reality of the cosmos. The Way is the ground of being, the direction of existence, the moral ethic of our actions, the hope of our future, and is very, very real. Though it's in all religions, it is far from any of the religion's superstitions or escapes. You can't pray to The Way for anything because it's there treating everything the same. There's no need to worship it because it is unimpressed and unaffected by what *we* say or want. It just is, and will always be, the wondrous uniting power at the base of the cosmos called The Way.

Making Bad Decisions

As I've said, evolving into a reflective state gives us the ability to reflect out and reflect in to *make our own decisions*. Rather than thinking and acting out of our inherited consciousness (or instinct), we are able to observe, make logical decisions and then act. I think it could be said that the principal thing that sets us apart as reflective beings (and is our calling) is to make logical, analyzed, good decisions...and we are not doing that. Most of our decisions are bad because of a decision that was first made around ten thousand years ago and has been held onto it ever since. It would be impossible to detail all of the bad decisions we've made since that time, though I will try to mention a few. I'll list first what I think is the most horrible decision we've made and still make, and I'll follow it with other bad decisions we've made as individuals, groups, and a species that keep us from seeing The Way.

1. The obvious worst decision we ever made was to discard and *not accept the powerful, necessary, connecting path of The Way, together with the parallel decision to replace it with the weak, disastrous, disconnecting path of pride.* These two decisions are the same, and they have totally altered who we are and where we're going. They are certainly the poster-child of all bad decisions, and we keep on making these decisions everyday. In fact I find that pride is at the core of most of our other bad decisions. Thus as long as we're submerged in pride, we will keep on making bad decisions until we reap the results of our destructive decision to become extinct. Yes, going extinct a very bad decision we make everyday, and it's our most ridiculous one, and all of these bad decisions deny us The Way.

2. Another decision that's right up at the top of bad decisions is when we *decide not to decide.* Making decisions should be natural to reflective beings, however it's not for us because are eaten up with pride. Many of us go through our lives making very few decisions or none at all. We just follow the person in front of us and do everything they say or do. This means that we never reflect or think for ourselves. That's why the bad decision of not making decisions totally blocks out our ability to enter The Way because you won't see it if you don't think for yourself. Pride is robbing us from thinking for ourselves, thinking outside the box, having any freedom of thought, or having any chance of making our own decisions. We just keep on moving through life blind to the lies of our pride-stuffed religions, societies, nations, and species, until we walk over the cliff.

3. We make horrible individual decisions everyday based on *our own needs*. We pretend that we are all that matters and we are the only one with needs. This separates and isolates us from other people, other groups, and other species. With pride at our base, our decision-making is inspired by fear, hate, selfishness, judging, and condemning to drive us apart. How anyone ever manages to get married, much less stay married, is a mystery to me, but keeping up relationships with friends, colleagues, or any one else has become increasingly impossible. Family connections are easier because we see these people as being like us and are thus more acceptable. (I believe that if we ever enter The Way, we will see every person and every species on the Earth as our family...because they really are.) Everyday we decide to compete with, fight, abuse, hurt, discredit, and even destroy other people and other species thinking it's the acceptable thing to do. These bad self-centered decisions are the main reason we're so lonely, messed up, depressed, miserable and left without purpose.

4. *Group-pride decisions* could be called the worst of the pride categories because they makes us paranoid about other sexes, races, cultures, societies, nationalities and religions. Group-pride works on and exaggerates our fears to make us choose divisive conflicts, violence and wars which wipe out the lives of millions, and leave the rest in poverty, sickness and hunger. What kind of a choice is that? We blindly buy into the prideful stereotypes of nationalism called patriotism, religious superiority, sexism, racism, the poor, and also the superiority of the rich and famous. The truth is that all groups are just made of people just like us, and all of these bad decisions deny that fact and rob us of The Way!

5. Though group-pride decisions are awful, but I believe that *species-pride decisions* are the worst. In them we decide everyday to destroy the Earth, the plants and other animals, the ecosystems that support all of life, and ourselves. All pride makes us insane, but species-pride goes beyond that; it makes us evil. What more can I say!

I hope that these comments on some bad decisions I've listed (there are countless more) make it clear how far off the track we've devolved, and how much we need to find The Way. It goes without saying that these bad decisions are blocking out The Way because

The Way is about coming together, and we're falling apart. If we could ever enter The Way, our decisions would be totally changed, and we would start moving together to be happy and real.

Not Embracing Evolution

I have no doubt that Charles Darwin, who first wrote about evolution, is the greatest scientist, or even thinker, of our time. In 1856, many years after he had visited the Galapagos Islands, he published his book on natural selection (not "random" selection which is nonsense and is used to describe it all the time). He talks about how the evolution of life on this Earth naturally (a word that refers to nature) moves froward by survival and reproduction. This includes multiple things like food, water, heat, cold, and other things that facilitate life. I find that this brilliant observation was just common sense, and if you think about it, you"ll agree. However because of pride-induced religious superstitions and resistance to change, Darwin was rejected and degraded by his peers, and this same ignorance is still going on today. This brilliant concept that first applied to the evolution of the Earth's species has now expanded out to be applied to everything, which is also revolutionary and inspiring.

We now know that the cosmos has been evolving ever since it first came into being with the Big Bang, and too often we ignore that too. We are not just a part of the cosmos; we *are* the cosmos. I've found it exciting to realize that everything, including ourselves, is evolving. Every movement, every change in our lives is a part of, and tied to, the great cosmic evolution. Our lives as a part of cosmic evolution evolve every day from childhood, to old age, and beyond. Each moment is a part of the evolution of this vast and powerful mystery. Though we fight it, nothing is ever the same from one second to next. Everything is constantly moving across the interconnected web of space/time within the cosmos to become something more complex and new.

This is essentially where traditional science stops because of its empirical (everything must be observed) approach to things and because a lot of scientists are pridefully locked into their own theories about the cosmos. To go further and ask deeper questions about the cosmos (which is a mystery) we have to depart from empiricism and turn to what might be called scientific philosophers such as the paleontologist Teilhard de Chardin who wrote a book called The Phenomenon of Man. He makes common sense observations such as the fact that *all* things in the cosmos must have some level of consciousness. He believes that some descending level of consciousness must be in all of evolving matter. This means that *Consciousness* is also evolving into complexity in the cosmos, just the same as matter. As things come together to become more complex in matter (atoms to molecules, molecules to cells, cells to bodies, leading ultimately to the complexity of the human brain), so consciousness comes together to grow in things like movement, thought, and reflective thought.

This growth in the complexity of consciousness we can clearly perceive in what we call "life". It can first be seen in the *movement* of cells. We can also see consciousness growing in complexity *up the ladder of life* to culminate in the jump of consciousness that we witness in the Homo sapiens brain's reflection. Thus evolution is not just *matter* moving into complexity through gravity; it is also *consciousness* moving into complexity through some other unnamed force.

What could that force be, and could we as humans have observed it? Could we even have given it a name? Yes, it's clear to me that what draws consciousness together is something we have experienced and found amazing. It is a force that is bringing all consciousness together throughout the cosmos (as does gravity in matter) to allow consciousness to grow more and more complex. We as humans have felt this amazing force in our reflective lives, and we have named it "*love*". Also we can now know that this force that brings consciousness together is one of the basic foundations of The Way which brings everything in the cosmos together..

Speaking of the word "force", let me digress to offer an example: I was captivated by the first Star Wars movie. One reason was because of George Lucas' concepts of what he called "The Dark Side" and "The Force". Of course in the movie the Dark Side was evil and The Force was good, and they were always confronting each other. This was the plot of the film. However I think this same thing is true of us. We are faced with a dark side that I call pride (and a lot of other words) with all of it's cruel satellites that lead to misery and death. However on the other hand, The Way with its satellites of love, humility, peace, etc. leads to life. Needless to say in <u>Star Wars</u> "The Force" is the strongest, just as The Way with its force of love is the strongest and will always win. (I'd love to talk about this some more, but I must be brief and move on.)

I believe from my research that the cosmos and evolution have a direction. All things (both matter and consciousness) are moving through The Way to become more complex to a place we can't possibly imagine. From our limitations of both time and space, there is no way that we could ever define where evolution is going. However we can see some indications of a direction as it advances. I also thinks this indicates that the cosmos may well have deep and presently unknown meaning. *(Pure, filtered, empirical science will not buy any of this because there is no empirical proof, but that doesn't mean that there is no truth to what I have just said. I think that without some logical speculation about things we cannot yet observe, we'll miss out on truths that will one day be empirically proven.)*

Each one of us is evolving even if we don't know it. Each minute, each day, each year of our lives we are evolving. Of course as reflective beings, we've now evolved to a complex, important point where we can make some choices. I don't think change should always be accepted, because change can either move us forward or backward to usher in both good and evil. However it is clear to me that with The Way we can move forward, because that's when we are coming together to be evolving in tune with the cosmos. Constantly moving together is how The Way leads the cosmos, and should be leading us to where we have to be.

Let me say again that unless we're evolving into The Way which moves us together, we will not be evolving forward. We won't be moving together with other people, other life forms, the Earth and the cosmos as the force of love tries to pull us. Instead we'll be moving apart into chaos and extinction to fall off the track of cosmic evolution as we *de*volve. At the same time as we evolve backward (which is what we're doing now in our pride, greed and arrogance), we automatically loose touch with The Way, our future, and our place on the Earth (all of which are grounded in the forward evolution of the cosmos). All the time in the cosmos there, beings have evolved that are out of tune with their surroundings, and the cosmos has had to discard them. That's what's happening to us now as we abuse the Earth, destroy our ecosystems, and kill off each other. The earth is being forced to slough us off because we have lost The Way.

I hope you can see there is no doubt that evolution is vitally important to us since it is who we are and can be. It's important that we not only accept it, but that we move together with The Way in our own evolution. We must embrace it every minute and encourage unity and peace to consciously flow. We must accept and even welcome the change that evolution brings, and not deny it or fight against it. Of course all of this is hard to do if we don't even know what evolution is. There is no denying that this common problem blocks our ability to see and enter The Way which moves us together in evolution's advance.

The gifts that evolution offers are huge. I think it's like Prometheus Unbound, an ancient Greek story by Aeschylus. It tells how Prometheus broke with the other selfish gods to give humanity fire. This gracious gift began the many human discoveries that followed, but it also put the rest of the gods into a jealous rage, so they condemned Prometheus to an eternity of suffering. It hit me that Prometheus in this story is a bit like evolution in our story, in that evolution is responsible for moving us forward from the past into the future to be a part of the cosmos. It too is what is freeing us to be these amazing reflective beings that can invent and grow. So obviously evolution should be celebrated and cherished rather than cast out and depicted as an enemy.

(If you want to know more about the subject of evolution, you can find it in Appendices IV at the end of the book.)

No Cosmos Consciousness

New information about the cosmos is constantly pouring in from the new and different telescopes. We now know that the cosmos is so vast that our human minds can't possibly wrap around it. Most of it we can't see or understand because we can't see out of our galaxy with its billions of stars that are all around us. I've mentioned before that we now know that we're a tiny dot on our planet, which is a tiny dot in this solar-system, which is a tiny dot in our galaxy, which is a microscopic dot in the cosmos. Everyday we learn more about the shocking number of planets that are revolving around the unknowable number of stars in the cosmos. This means that we can now conclude that there are millions or perhaps billions of planets out there that not only could have life, but could also have reflective life! Also everyday we learn more about things like black holes, quasars, pulsars, nebulae and all the other growing wonders of the cosmos from whence we've come.

It was not that long ago that we had a world view that said the Earth was a kind of super-dome with stars at the top of the roof (along with various gods and spirits), the sun beneath them moving across the sky during the day and the moon moving across at night.... and that was it. We may smile when we think about that, but many people today are still stuck in an outmoded world view. They still see themselves and all people in general as being the center and pinnacle of everything, and see the Earth as being the only planet that's important in the cosmos. Very few have broken out of this ancient picture to absorb any of the things we now know of the cosmos, and thus they can't evolve to update who they really are. I have had several people say to me that they didn't want to talk about the cosmos, because "it's just too scary". What they mean is that they don't want to give up any of their easy, simplistic, self-centered world view. They don't want to accept that we aren't really the center of anything, much less the cosmos, and that we're only a teeny tiny part of some unknown, amazing everything...which when you think about it, is not so bad.

Now what does this have to do with The Way? Having a "cosmos consciousness" first of all makes us humble, and being humble is basic to The Way. If we are all caught up in ourselves and in our prideful illusions of self- importance, we can't possibly appreciate The Way because it has to do with the importance and well-being of everyone and everything. The Way is about love, compassion, sharing, giving, and all the other things we've talked about. Certainty these things don't sit well with a world view that can only picture, "me, me, me". We need to update ourselves by updating our view of the cosmos if we are going enter The Way to survive as a species. It's clear to me that because of our pride and arrogance that's wiping out our cosmos consciousness, we are blocking The Way.

There may be nothing that blocks The Way more than our ignorance and lack of education about the evolution of the Earth and cosmos. This gaping hole in our knowledge is a central player in our blind drift into extinction. Our basic ignorance coming from our poor education on the Earth and cosmos is absolutely tragic because we are not teaching about who we really are. I'll talk more about this later.

Shallow Motivations and Goals

Our motivations and goals are buried in pride's self-centered ways to limit any real reflection on them. When I've asked people what motivates them, they've said things like making lots of money or pleasing their parents, spouses, Gods or everybody. Some said their motivation was to go to heaven and stay out of hell. All of these things revolve around nothing but me, me, me, so there's no recognition that other people or anything else matters or even exists. Of course this is to be expected from a species that worships pride to leave us buried within ourselves. Our motivations and goals reflect this tragedy, and we shout it out with our actions. We need to dramatically expand the scope of our motivations and goals not just to include other people, but to include everything including the cosmos. We need to come out of this isolated, uncaring, self-centered no dark cave of violence and war, and look around. When we do, we'll see that we are not the only or even the best person, race, nationality, class or anything else. We'll also see that we're not the only species on this planet that matters since there are still thousands of other species that we have not yet destroyed. We're also not the only planet, solar system, or galaxy out there, since there are unknown numbers of others that we'll never be able to see or know anything about.

The point is that we need to widen the scope of our motivations and goals to bring them up to date to include and access The Way.

For instance, if our motivation or goal involves money, it should not just be money for our own benefit, but money for the benefit and well-being of every person, every life form and the Earth itself. If our motivation is to please someone, we should expand it to please everyone and everything. Really everything we do should be for the benefit of everything that exists in the cosmos

I know this kind of thinking sounds strange, but if it's true that we're interconnected to each other, the Earth and the cosmos, shouldn't our goals and motivations reflect that fact? Also shouldn't we be motivated to keep-up and protect the Earth,,,no, shouldn't we be motivated to *advance* the Earth? Shouldn't we be advancing the Earth's ecosystems and evolution? In the same way, shouldn't we not just study and try to understand the cosmos and its evolution,, but shouldn't we seek ways to advance their discovery by advancing their education? Although our knowledge of the cosmos is limited and we can know very little about it, we can still struggle to advance our own understanding as new discoveries are released, and be open to participate in and give thanks for the endless wonders of the cosmos that is responsible for who we are.

I think what I'm really trying to say is that widening our perspective on everything should dramatically affect our goals and motivations. All of our perspectives (on a personal, group, national, world, or species level) need to be lifted to advance our motivations and goals to perceive The Way. The Way is not about us; it's about everything, and it is the moral ethic that underlies everything in the whole cosmos. Our goals and motivations need to come from our recognizing that we are interconnected to everything and having an open mind with a wider perspective. There is no doubt that self-centered, arrogant, prideful motivations and goals dramatically block our ability to appreciate and accept of The Way, which is understood through a liberated reflection that has cast off pride.

I said before that being reflective is when we have enough awareness through our complex minds to reflect out to perceive what's around us, and reflect in to understand ourselves. Thus this ability should by now have allowed us, in our evolution, to see The Way, enter it and become it. We should already understand and know that only in The Way will we find the security, peace, community, and future we desperately need and long for. It should by now be clear that The Way is a part of all reflective, cosmic evolution now evolving into being throughout the cosmos and is more than a bunch of words, ideas, or postulations.

In other words right now The Way should be our central goal and motivation, but we're so far from that reality that this statement sounds silly. However The Way is still around, and it will always remain right here. Other reflective beings after we're gone, who evolve on this planet or other planets in the cosmos will have motivations and goals grounded in The Way. They will to be able to accept The Way's wisdom to continue the evolution of this new, exciting, complex being we call reflective. The Way never leaves us, but everyday we are leaving The Way.

Our Thinking Bubbles

Another realization that can help us to be open to The Way is to see that we live in learned, non-reflective, thinking bubbles. Some of these bubbles may occasionally have something about them that is good, but most of them are just, plain bad. They separate us from other people, from other ways of thinking, from other cultures, and from our ability to think for ourselves.

For instance, we generally begin life living in family bubbles. They teach us the rules and mores of our nuclear or extended families, but mostly they just teach us what our parents think. As we grow up, we find ourselves in other mental bubbles such as regional, national, political, religious, racial, occupational, social, educational or work bubbles. Most of us are so caught up in our bubbles within bubbles that we never look out, look around, and think for ourselves. We never get around to using our brains (as they're meant to be used) to reflect and search for the truth. In one sense we're slaves to our bubbles as we blindly exist only believing and following what's right there in front of us.

Can we break out of these thinking bubbles? I'm more optimistic about that than you might think. I really do believe that we can get out of many of them, and some people do it. Many of those people have had dramatic experiences that have helped them to get out.

Others accomplish it through education, travel or just being honest. Some find a friend that they trust who has broken out to help others do the same...but it's not easy.

However we have to admit that releasing ourselves from our limiting, confining bubble-prisons to think for ourselves is far too rare. That's one of the main reasons we have so many stupid and unnecessary problems in the world. We are always stuck in prideful bubbles that keep telling us, "my thinking bubbles are better than yours". For instance we say that my culture is the only culture; my religion is the only religion; or my nation and even species is the only one that matters. Obviously this leaves us awash in discord, division, violence, war, and a questionable future. These bubbles leave us blind to reality, disconnected, lonely and afraid, retreating into places that aren't there.

I'm convinced that the first step in getting out of our thinking bubbles is to recognize them. If we can see them and recognize them for what they are, we can begin to find ways to pop them, think for ourselves, and be real. As we come out of our stale, dark, bubble-caves, we find ourselves facing the invigorating fresh air of truth that allows everyone to be who they really are, and possibly allow mother Earth (with her many life forms) to be who she really is too. What a beautiful thing it is to depart from this prideful bubble-worship to begin a new life open to the wonder of freely, honestly thinking for ourselves about all that is evolving in us and around us, and tasting the fresh air of our interconnections with everyone and everything. This can allow us to rejoice not just in ourselves, but in the wonder of everything evolving in the unknowable cosmos of which we're a part.

Obviously unless we can get out of our thinking bubbles, we won't be able to see The Way because the way is presently lost to most of us . If all we'll do is follow the massive thinking bubbles of pride to follow the ones right in front of us, we are lost. We will only think and live going around in mindless bubble-circles that are devoid of The Way..

Our Unethical Social Order

We've established that we are a part of the Earth's evolution that has gone off track, and that is because we worship pride to not know what humility means. Of course this is constantly reflected in how we act and in what we do. All of our communities, nations, institutions, and even our educational systems have been warped by pride's sick presence. Thus injustice is everywhere so that4 any concern for the interconnected common-good is difficult to find.

Nothing makes this more clear than our terrible system of exchange. It was first used in trade (trading this for that to get food and other necessities), and then it evolved into the notes and coins we call "money," This money no more has to do with our having what's necessary or need, but it now has to do with our greed in accumulating more and more of it. It's become a fear driven ego game where we constantly try to accumulate all the money we can get...and more. I think this senseless accumulation of unnecessary funds and the injustice of the resulting money distribution (where the poor get poorer and the rich get richer) has perhaps become the most divisive, mean, and self-centered thing of pride's takeover. We just accept and approve that a few people control most of the world's wealth as they pile up millions or billions of dollars, to leave others living in poverty and even starvation.

Is their anything ethical about this? How can we not see that our money distribution system is unjust, unethical and sick? This is a giant bubble of insanity that we find in all nations to make them devoid of compassion, decency and common sense. All religions have warned about the temptations and potential evils of money, while then supporting this unjust money system. Some more realistic, sensible way of dispersing the world's wealth must be found to reward people justly for their hard work if we are ever to embrace of interconnected state and come close to seeing and entering The Way.

Another example of the unethical social order that I often talked about, is the dominant culture of militarism and war that sees the horrors of war as not only acceptable but as commendable, heroic, and even holy. How can this be? How can a reflective, intelligent species build a culture around violence and murder and think it's good? Is it really good to spend a major part of the world's resources on preparing for and waging wars that throw away the lives of countless youth? Militarism, war, and murder are never good, and that fact is recognized in every religion and everybody else with common sense. War is evil, and I believe deep down we know that, but we still get pumped up by our national and cultural pride to throw common sense out the window...and The Way too.

These are a few of the things that make up our unethical social order. We should also mention things like the mass incarceration of our penal systems, the racially biased courts, and our money-run politics, our biased health care systems, and our limited, unequal school and college availability. Once again we all know that these things are bad, but since all we really care about is accumulating money, we just don't care...and do nothing. We are a divided, fighting, weary species that's lost in unethical confusion that leave us blindly stumbling through our pride-soaked lives into extinction... and needless to say, we avoid and miss The Way.

One reason we accept this is that most people think that this is our only option. I hear things like: "Everybody does it; I don't want to look different or silly; I don't want to rock the boat; I want to fit in." Thus we live on in our misery awaiting our demise, accepting a culture of guns violence, militarism, war, poverty and starvation, and always being mean. We live in unethical, lost societies without thinking about what we're doing. Sure occasionally somebody speaks out against injustice, but they're usually ignored or called naive, weird, traitors or something worse.

Obviously all of this has nothing to do with The Way, because The Way is made up of truth, decency, kindness, love and peace that bring us together rather than tear us apart. There is no doubt that our unethical social order blocks The Way. However, as I've said, we still have our reflective capabilities that are capable of leading us out of this mess, so all we've got to do is start using them and we will find The Way.

Lost Respect for the Earth

A huge block to our being able to see the way is our shocking loss of respect for (and identification with) the Earth and its many life forms. We have lost our natural sense of connection to the Earth and everything. Some people are today rediscovering the fact of our connection to the Earth in our discussions of ecosystems, but it should be obvious to us that *everything* is connected to everything. This means that to only be interested in, and concerned about, ourselves (which is what pride teaches) is both preposterous and dangerous.

For most of our Homo sapiens evolution, we not only respected the Earth – we worshiped it. We should remember that the word "worship" was first identified around 1200 AD coming from the Old English Anglican word "wurthscip" which meant accepting something as worthy. Later around 1338, the word "wurshipe" appeared to refer to something supernatural or divine. Thus the wonder, adoration and sense of worth felt by our ancestors for the Earth and its life forms, became replaced by divine beings in the sky. What I'm saying here is that our ancestors did not worship the Earth in the same way that we worship our various gods; rather they revered and offered thanks to the Earth, and all of its other inhabitants, for giving them life, sustenance, and community.

However we've lost all of that, and it's destroying us. We're not only ignoring the Earth, but many even see it as our enemy. This shocking disrespect for this obvious mother and provider we call Earth has been devastating to us. The reasons we've done this are many, but they all revolve around the rise of our arrogant pride.

Look at this mess – with our unchecked population we are swarming the Earth like locusts to pollute everything with trash. toxins and plastics, and we are wiping out all of the plants and animals everywhere. Three of the most destructive things that we ignore are our overpopulation, our increasing use of non-biodegradable plastics, and our increasing use and pollution of fresh water to make it so scarce that it has already killed thousands. These abuses of the Earth are big players in the pollution that is major part of our unfolding predicament. I think that the most ignored is overpopulation which is caused by too many births and our tremendous advances in medical science. This obviously is multiplying our pollution and speeding-up the destruction of our ecosystems. It is also progressively driving us crazy in over-crowded cities, roads, and everything else to reduce our sense of well-being and sanity.

Parallel to these things is our rampant industrialization using the easy energy of oil and coal for fuel. The power-plants and other big businesses are polluting more and more, and they even encourage more overpopulation to up our spending to advance our sacred "progress". Absolutely no thought is given to any responsibility for this planet and its ecosystems of which we are a part. It is really weird when we say that animals need to be neutered to control their numbers, but we don't. We especially need to be neutered as we swarm the earth to destroying the animals and everything else. A few people have recognized that we are polluting the land, water and air to destroy the delicate balance of our ecosystems, but recognizing and doing something about it are two different things, so no one really does anything.

The recent rise of an exchange we call "money" has replaced our home the Earth as that to which we ascribe worth (worship). Money with its greed is blocking any actions to reverse what we're doing to the environment. Thus there is no indication that anything will change, so we're left to conclude that we will soon eliminate our species (and most of the other species) to not have a home.

Obviously none of this bears any resemblance to The Way, because The Way has to do with humility, love, peace, etc. and that is totally lost in this horrible, dark picture we're painting. Is it any wonder that The Way, which is natural to us, has become lost because of an unnatural thing that is leaving us warped, confused and miserable? We're adrift in a sea of anger, cruelty, fear and violence as we cruelly abuse of the Earth to our end. There is no question that we're totally lost!

I would never say that there is no hope, because reflective beings are designed to be reflective, and also because we can't predict the future. However I would say, from all of the evidence that I've found, together with numerous scholarly works I've read, that the future of our species is bleak. Extinction will happen not just to us, but to any other reflective species in the cosmos that looses sight of The Way to evolves apart rather than evolving together...being connected rather than being disconnected...being loving and humble rather than being arrogant and prideful. The Way is the glue that is meant to hold all reflective species together, and when, as we have done, it's cast aside, everything falls apart.

Let me repeat that our being interconnected to the Earth and everything else may be the most important thing for us to embrace. We're a part cosmos and the earth with its ecosystems, and species. We are intertwined with all that is. Let me give you an example: a recent article in National Geographic reports a study of how the atmosphere carries pollution swiftly from one place to another all over the world. For instance pictures from a satellite show pollution traveling from China to the west coast of the U.S., and then over all of North America in only a few days. This means that unless *all* countries stop pollution, no country will stop pollution. (Most people have no knowledge about global warming or ecosystems.) We must quickly learn how connected we are on the Earth and how sacred and precious the Earth is to us.

(If you think I'm exaggerating our pending extinction, read a scientific report in Appendix V at the end of the book.)

Loss of Awe and Spirituality

We have discussed this a little, but I feel it deserves more attention. Let me say that I'm not talking about spirituality in the same way that most religions address it. I'm not talking about having mystical communications or interactions with some divine being. I know that this is valued by many people and brings them comfort, but I'm not there. My interpretation of spiritual is the feeling of awe, wonder and interaction that I have with the Earth and the cosmos. However because of things like superstitions, scientific scorn, the greed of money, and downright ignorance, we have lost this powerful and uplifting experience of awe, wonder and belonging because in our pride, all we are able to see is ourselves.

I consider myself to be a mystic, but mystics have had a terrible press because they're often falsely associated with things like alchemy or magic. The truth is that mystics are found in all religions and other places that are aware of the mystery within us and outside us. Mystics are aware that we know only a microscopic amount about things like our minds, the Earth and the cosmos. We do know that these things exist because our limited senses tell us that they do, but beyond that, we know very little about them or much of anything. Thus it's logical that we should stand in awe of life and nature and relate to them in a spiritual way. Our loss of awe and spirituality is really a sad and grieving development.

I realize that if you look up the word "spiritual" in the dictionary, it says it's about religion. I used to think of it that way, but I've come to realized that I'm connected to, and a part of, some vast, unknowable everything. I've also realized that I *am* that "vast everything" and that "vast everything" is me! I experience spirituality through a mixture of wonder, thanksgiving and awe, as I see that we are interconnected to, and dependent upon, each other, all other species, the Earth, the Sun and the cosmos. Yes, we are interconnected to, a part of, and are everything in the mighty cosmos with its endless immensity and shocking power. As happens to some people in their response to a religion, I find that just the experience of being reflective, alive, and evolving makes me feel blessed and spiritual.

I feel spiritual when I am able to get out out of our overpopulated chaos and feel the earth and its multitude of species as was done by our ancient descendants. I love trees as the wind blows through them and the birds ever amazing concerts within them. I love to walk in the mountains or on the beach when no people are around to distract me. As I've said, our ancestors had a spiritual connection with the Earth its animals, its plants, as well as the wondrous sky with its Sun and stars. They understood essentially nothing about them (as is still true with us), but they had enough wisdom to approach them with awe and wonder. The loss of this spiritual approach to life I believe is a major player in our decent into the pride-worship that makes us believe that we can control and know everything about them and use it to our selfish advantage.

Also I've found that The Way itself is spiritual in that it fills us with awe as it guides everything together, and, when we enter it, ourselves as well It's clear to me that one of the reasons we've discarded The Way is because of our lost spirituality It's also clear that our loss of reverence for the things our senses and reflection reveal to us, has blocked out The Way. We've lost The Way's mystical presence that's always right there. If we rediscover and enter The Way, we'll rediscover our lost spiritual side that includes humility, love and knowing peace.

Making Our Myths Human

In our pride and selfishness as Homo sapiens, we are constantly trying to make things over in our own image. We take it as an insult if everything is not exactly like us. Of course the truth is that nothing is just like us, just as no other species is just like our species. Animals and plants are close to us on the evolutionary ladder, but they're not just like us. Our anthropomorphic need to make everything human clearly comes from our being totally self-centered. It's just another example of our arrogant insanity.

Perhaps the most problematic place we find this anthropomorphic zeal is in our religious myths. For instance, we try to turn *our* thoughts about a "Creator", "Source", or "Divine Presence" into a absolute fact, and say that these mythological things are exactly like us. We make the myths about our gods human. Many religions have put these mythological figures up in the sky where they say that *their* gods are like a mighty king looking down to rule over his court and control everything. It is also listening to each person to answers their requests and give them special blessings. Each of us says that "my" divine concept is superior to all of the other gods that people have. Thus we demand that everyone change their myths to be just like ours...and if they don"t, we try to convince them to change, or get mad and cast them out of our lives to persecute them...and sometimes go to war.

We also pridefully say that because *we* are such a special special species with such a special divine being, we will live right on and on after death and not die like the animals and plants. This goes with another anthropomorphic act where we conclude that after death *we* are going to a good place with gold streets where we will be eternally happy, but those who don't agree with us are evil and will go to a bad place of fire and pain where everyone is eternally miserable. Some religions talk about how we can come back after death to be born as something else depending on how we've previously lived. All of this is about the subject of death, and the truth is we know absolutely nothing about it, because none of us have ever been there, Still we can't even resist putting our human stamp on death.

Let me also mention our tendency to take religious writings and declare them to be "holy". Of course *my* religious writings, that have been dictated by a divine source, are more important than your religious writings since mine come straight from the Divine. We can see this in most religious writings (such as the Torah, Bible, Qur'an and others). Of course these writings are not only made holy, but they are worshiped, revered and turned into idols. I could go on with further examples of our anthropomorphic acts, but hopefully this is enough to make the point that we are obsessed with pridefully making our myths human.

The reason I think this practice blocks The Way is because I've found that many of the teachings of the world's religions did *originally teach The Way*. However soon after their beginnings, prideful superstitions and myths evolved to take them over. For instance I fully believe from my research that The Buddha taught The Way from the Hindu perspective of the within, while Jesus taught The Way from the Jewish perspective of the without, but in reality they were both teaching the same thing...they were both teaching The Way. However at this point, even though we claim that modern Buddhism came straight from Buddha, and modern Christianity came straight from Jesus, most of what is now left, even in their scriptures, has come from the later additions of anthropomorphic superstitions coming from our pride.

These myths of human likeness have taken us over to block us from seeing who we really are and from taking The Way seriously. They have distracted and turned us away from what might have been a humble, connected life full of love and real relationships that are evolving together in tune with the cosmos. Now we are stuck in fearful, judgmental lives of superstition, pride and disconnectedness . We have lost our ancestors awe for the Earth and the cosmos as we annihilate the ecosystems to kill ourselves and most other life forms. Sometimes our religious superstitions are used to block our willingness to address the fact that we are moving into extinction polluting the air, water and land and killing off the Earth's animals and plants to destroy the ecosystems. People say that we have nothing to do with it because the world belongs to their god and he will take care of it.

If we are to see and step into The Way, we've got to get back on track to embrace things that are real and true...and what I see as being real and true is the Earth and the cosmos and not a bunch of anthropomorphic myths that do nothing but distract us. We must embrace the now camouflaged cosmic ethical and moral system that is called The Way which is who we really are, and who we have to be. We've got to wake up and be real in the real and inspiring presence of The Way.

Killing Any Life Form

I feel quite strongly about this one because most people don't seem to care that we live in a killing culture. Killing has become such a natural and accepted part of who we are that it's frightening. For instance, we mostly eat food that has been killed; we enthusiastically support the enlistment of young people who are taught to kill and then sent off to war to die; we love plays, movies, television shows and video games about war and murder; and one of our popular sports is killing animals for no reason.

The killing of other people or animals has become so ingrained in our culture that it's become a part of who we are. At one time in our evolution, it was necessary for us to kill other animals to have food and protect ourselves. However as reflective beings, we should have long ago evolved out of killing both animals and plants, because we could easily survive (as do our fellow mammals called whales) on the least complex one celled life forms on the Earth like plankton. We might have sensed the sacredness of all life if we had not blindly overpopulated the Earth to demand more and more food for more and more people, and if we had not lost our minds in unsustainable energy to pollute everything. I spoke earlier about what the act of killing does to people in wars that causes a shocking rise in suicides. This same wounding of the soul has happened to groups of people such as the United States' history of slavery or Germany's slaughter of the Jews. Mass killings (especially in wars) take a lot of time to heal, and they probably never heal at all.

Many people seem to compassionately think that we can stop killing animals by becoming vegetarians or vegans, but the only way we can stop the murder of both animals and vegetation for humanity's mass consumption is to first *stop our overpopulation*. Let me repeat, we must return to numbers below 750 million to allow the ecosystems of the Earth to revive and work naturally. We must stop fighting nature and work with it to allow its ecosystems to be balanced and free of our egotistical, selfish, money-driven overpopulation and meddling. Only then will we be able to stop killing off the Earth's animals and vegetation....and only then can we be free of the terrible guilt of our present abuse and murder of all life. This would also allow us to move closer together (and enter The Way) instead of moving further apart in pride. We are now shutting off our reflective abilities as we continue to murder each other and our brother and sister species within the Earth's evolution.

We've talked about this before, but let me share with you something personal about how killing psychologically effects us. After struggling with our dear cat Bubba's kidney dysfunction, my wife and I were recently forced to go to a vet to have him put down. We stayed in the room while he trustfully looked up into our eyes and died from the vet's shot. I didn't know that it would affect me so dramatically, but it leveled me. I could hardly sleep for several days. If that's how I felt putting my cat to sleep, how do you think I would feel if I killed a fellow human being? Thank goodness I have not had to do that, but vast numbers of others have.

I do not believe that war is the answer to anything either for this country or for the world. I'll admit that if conditions are really extraordinary (as they were in World War II) defending ourselves as a last resort might be necessary. However World War I began from a misunderstanding and was nothing but a egotistical, diplomatic disaster that should never have happened. The same was true for the more recent wars in Vietnam (for fear of communism), Afghanistan (because the Taliban government wouldn't turn over Asama Ben Laden when they had no idea where he was) or of course Iraq (because some people thought Sudham Hussein had nuclear weapons).

It is historically clear that most wars can be avoided if we can just set aside our national pride that is always driving the nations to demand their own way rather than discussing and negotiating. We must also stop the prideful practice of grabbing other nation's ground, rather than seeking common ground. No one wins a war. Everyone looses. We all know that...but driven by our pride (with its fear, anger, greed and need for power), we continue on with this sickening nightmare of mass murder! The effects that killing has on people has been proved by the number of suicides and nervous breakdowns people have when they return to their regular lives after being trained to kill people and have then done so. This goes against some deeply embedded ethic within, and I think that ethic is The Way.

The Way is found in most religions and people with common-sense, and it cries out "Do Not Kill". When we don't follow that advice, it is never erased from our psyche, because the truth is that killing is unacceptable, whether we kill another human or anything else. This means we should never kill any life form, especially those on the higher level of life's evolutionary ladder like animals and plants. When we do kill something, we pay for it mentally, and we also push further away the ability to see or become The Way. That's why I believe that our insistence on keeping guns (whose only purpose is to kill something) and our worship of militarism and war (whose results are always sickening) are responsible for so many of our health problems because killing anesthetizes our souls.

Poor Education

Education is where we pass on to the next generation the accumulation (or evolution) of our knowledge. This should not just be knowledge that comes from the distant past (because most of it is very valuable), but it should especially be knowledge that comes from the present that has only recently been released. If we don't keep up with educational advances, we'll block the evolution of wisdom and truth from ourselves and for the next generation. Thus we *must* constantly struggle to keep our education moving on...we must keep it evolving. This is especially true in these times when so much new knowledge is emerging because of the new ways we have to communicate. Sometimes there's a temptation to just give up and say there is just too much of it...it's just too hard...but we can't. It's vitally important to us and those who follow us; so we must hang on and keep trying! As reflective beings, it's our responsibility and our calling to understand as much as we can about ourselves and all that's around us, and then pass it on. If we don't do that, we've failed.

I have mentioned the explosion of knowledge that has come recently within both science and religion (with all the new translations of world religions), but the same thing is true at all levels of education. Every day there are new and exciting revelations in our paths that demand our immediate attention. Passing this on both past and present wisdom should be one of our top priorities, but tragically it is not.

Education is even being attacked by many as they try to live in the past and hang onto outmoded, prejudiced ideas. Education is pushed to the back-burner to make room for militaristic, financial, superstitious matters of pride that drain and even attack real, necessary education. The ignorance coming from our lack of education stands behind a lot of our problems as it minimizes our lives now and our chance to have a future.

My wife and I just came back from a visit to Canada where we found the people there to be very friendly and relaxed. We saw no indication of crime on the streets, and even with only banning automatic weapons and tightening gun controls, shootings were not a problem because out of common sense, nobody carries guns around anymore. The level of trust and cooperation was amazing to me, so we asked one of our guides why they thought this was so. They said that at one time Canada had one of the worst literacy and crime rates in the world. Chaos was everywhere and the people were frustrated and unhappy.

A new, progressive, charismatic, prime minister came into office who asked the government to do an in-depth analysis of the situation and make dramatic suggestions. Almost overnight they changed their educational system to make it a top priority at all levels of government. Soon everybody in Canada was given an equal, solid education, and it was expected that *everyone* would attend school through high-school. Also a college education was encouraged by making cheap, national colleges available all over the country. The whole budget was amended to make education the top priority in every province of the country.

In the following years, things quickly began to change. Of course literacy was soon at a very high level, but also crime plummeted, and cooperation and the economy flourished. My source said that now the people of Canada are more inclusive, secure, and free to grow than they ever were before. She said that they still have some problems, but everyone was excited about how far they had come. Needless to say, it was an eye-opening chat, and we really enjoyed our visit.

This reminds me of something else: I've always found that any of my trips to another country and culture were a truly eye-opening, educational experience. Education is not confined to books or classrooms; it also comes from listening and learning everywhere, and it certainly comes from travel. Marc Twain said, "Travel is fatal to bigotry, prejudice and narrow-mindedness". Many of the places in which I taught required at least one semester abroad to graduate. That's because foreign travel is one of the best teachers. I grieve that the United States is so cut off from the rest of the world that most people only travel around within it, because traveling to other countries opens us to new cultures, ideas, and people that opens up our minds and souls. There is no question that a person is robbed of that experience when they don't travel abroad.

I mentioned earlier that most people don't know or care about the Earth or the cosmos that makes up who we are because they've never been taught about them. All they know about is making money, raising families, and supporting their governments in waging wars and their religious superstitions (which often discourage accepting science). Reflecting honestly on nature and cosmology to see where we come from and where we're going is seen as a silly waste of time, and is sometimes even called pagan. Thus we continue our devolution into the void of ignorance. I think our education about the Earth and the cosmos should not just be taught in schools but be a thing we see everyday as a top priority. It is necessary for us to be up to date in understanding ourselves and our surroundings. Also if we are to have a future,we must have a clear understanding of the Earth's ecosystems. How many people know anything about the ecosystems? Very few, because they've never been taught this basic aspect of who we are. In this area and many others, education is tragically lacking as people learn more and more about selfish trivia...about how to be rich, how to fight wars, how great their nation and religion are, and all of the other "practical" things.

The Way is a complicated subject, and if it is to be understood in these blind "me, me, me" times, we have to break out of the norm. I believe that education is one of our best tickets out of our self-chosen addiction to pride. Education can launch us into new dimensions of understanding and reason to see things we've never imagined before. It can definitely help us to see The Way...to see the obvious, moral ethic that is at the core of the cosmos and each one of us. Thus to ignore and block education is to ignore and block The Way, and to ignore and block The Way is now leading us into the misery and extinction that is right in front of us.

Lost Appreciation of Beauty

This one may surprise you, but I do believe that when we lose our appreciation of beauty, we also block The Way. To see and appreciate beauty means that we are open to the pleasing and appealing things that exist around us. It means that we're not so lost in negative trivialities and the denial of our positive emotions that we're still able to appreciate the beauty that comes from seeing, hearing, smelling, touching and all of our intuitive senses. It means that positive emotions and responses that come from recognizing that kind people and our place in the amazing cosmos are still a part of who we are. It means that we're not so closed within ourselves that we can't look out to see and feel the beauty of a sunset, a landscape, a painting, some appealing music (as we appreciate the beautiful sounds of the vibrating human vocal cords or fine instruments) as well as beautiful writings and ideas. It means that we're still in touch with the underlying beauty of everything to rejoice within it. It means that our soul has not been so tarnished or washed away by the dark influence of pride that it is lost. *(I believe the word "soul" could mean "The Way" that is still there to make us real.)*

Ugliness is seeing things as bad, whereas beauty is seeing those things as good. As they say, "Beauty is in the eye of the beholder." This quote could mean that if we can't see the beauty around us, we've lost sight of, and become blind to, the goodness,

reality, truth and The Way within it. (Incidentally, this blindness analogy can be found in the original writings of most religions to indicate the darkness of the soul.)

Of course this quote can also mean that people appreciate beauty in different ways. For instance, some people like classical music, while others like jazz, rock or country. Some people like traditional paintings, while others like expressionistic or modern ones. We're all slightly different, and it comes out in the way we appreciate the various inputs of our senses, but for any of us to lose sight of what we have in common, and loose our appreciation of things like nature, love, compassion, and life, is just tragic...but that's where most of us are today. In relationship with other people, our sick society stresses outward beauty (most of which comes from our genes), rather than inward beauty (which has to do with who we really are). To be open to beauty is too often missing in our lives, because we never have the time or inclination to be open to it.

As I said, beauty is found in different things in different ways. Beauty can be found in just living everyday. We forget that life does not make us angry, *we* make ourselves angry at life. Life is what life is – an evolution that has been given to us from the Earth and the cosmos. We are born and we die, and if we could ever get out of our prideful anger, worry, guilt, judging, comparing, greed, and superior egos, we would see that life is amazing...and that life is beautiful. It's our pride-filled ways of looking at life that make us feel angry and miserable with life. If we could move into the power of The Way, we would be able to rejoice in the incredible beauty of all things. It's obvious to me that losing our ability to know and appreciate beauty in its many forms is one of the major blocks to knowing The Way.

No Honesty and Truth

Honesty and truth are two sides of the same coin. Honesty is generally thought to be about how individuals speak to each other, but it has to do with many other things. For instance, groups like nations can be dishonest (and there is an epidemic of that), religions can be dishonest, and what we say about other races, sexes, political parties as well as nations and religions is frequently dishonest. To be dishonest is to say or do something which, deep down, we know is not good or true. To be truthful is the same. Reflected beings are made to search for the truth, to speak the truth, and to live the truth. The truth and being honest should always be our goals.

However that is not where pride has taken us. We now focus only on ourselves when in reality we are interconnected to, and a part of, everything. Thus we are being dishonest and untruthful about who we are and are living a lie. We have become untruthful and dishonest with ourselves as we follow the path of pride, since obviously we are not the only thing that is important in the cosmos. Also we are not superior to, or the only thing that matter in the cosmos! All that pride teaches is a lie, and I think deep down we know that and are confused and miserable about it. I have spoken elsewhere about what the real truth of who we are is, so I won't do that here, but it is true that lies about our superiority are destroying us, because our species pride-lie is ruining us and the Earth.

Of course our dishonesty and lying also distance us from The Way that could brings us together to experience honesty and truth if we gave it a chance. In fact to be dishonest flies in the face of everything The Way stands for. Dishonesty insults The Way because the way is real (which is another word for honest). However we have evolved to cheat, lie and commit fraud without thinking about it all the time.

Children learn that they can more effectively get what they want if they lie, so lying becomes natural to most small children. However the reason they don't quickly grow out of this is because they start seeing the grown-ups around them lying. Soon they are following their role models in their prideful, lying ways. They do this instead of sensibly stopping lying when they evolve to understand their connection to and responsibility for others. Soon they advance in their lying to become experts in it that further contributes to our mess.

Can you imagine what our relationships would be like if honesty and truth were a central part of who we are? Can you imagine what the world would be like if honesty and truth were a part of the nations politics and foreign policy? Our lives would certainly change dramatically for the good and our relationships would blossom. Also, of course, we would make a major jump toward The Way as we evolved into the cosmos.

Fill your bowl to the brim
and it will spill.
Keep sharpening your knife
and it will blunt.
Chase after money and security
and your heart will never unclench.
Care about people's approval
and you will be their prisoner.
Do your work, then step back,
It's the only path to serenity. Tao te Ching

IV Word Paths to The Way

The following words I'll offer are not The Way, however I can say that they are paths to, or parts of, a human attempt to describe The Way. Light and heat are not the Sun, but light and heat indicate that the Sun is there. Crashing waves are not the ocean but they indicate that the vast ocean is near. The beautiful songs of birds are not birds, but they tell us that the birds are near. In the same way these word-paths are not The Way, but they indicate the unifying presence of The Way, that exists all around us and within us, is real and gives us hope. Thus I find these words to be very valuable because they serve as paths to help us find The Way...which is no small thing!

I'm just saying that we should not look at these words as being something in themselves, but as something that points to so much more. I call them word-paths because they can lead us to The Way. If you let yourself get bogged down in any of these words, reading this will not only be boring, but you'll totally miss the goal. It will distract you from why they're being mentioned, which is to help you see, understand and enter into the cosmos' complex, huge and wonderful ethic.. The Way is what's important and not any words.

What makes these words powerful is the fact that they are all talking about something that is *bringing us together!* These are all words that defy pride's attempts to disconnect us, as they point us to something that gives us back our intended evolutionary path of being connected and at peace. Look at the words; think about them; and see that all of them try to bring us together. As I saw these words spill out in the statements of the Parliament of World Religions, this became clear to me. I also saw that what is behind these words is a force that is trying to bring us together to be who we really are...a unifying force that offers us meaning, purpose, joy and a future.

We'll begin this with the two powerful word-paths called *love and humility*, because I consider these two word-paths to be the foundation and core of The Way. I also feel that these two words go hand in hand. You can't have humility without love, and you can't have love without humility. Humility and love hold each other together to allow them to grow. Whenever we say anything about one, we're automatically saying it about the other. They're not just twins; they're conjoined (or Siamese) twins. If we didn't deal with these two word-paths first, then any further discussion of The Way would be difficult if not impossible, because all of the other word-paths lean on them. They hold the others up and allow them to exist and continue.

We'll start with humility because I've written a book about it called <u>The Absurdity of Pride and the Peace of Humility</u> (which of course I recommend), and also because humility has become lost to us. Most people don't even know what the word means. However it's a fact that finding humility can dramatically change our lives, because it means we are throwing off pride (its opposite) with its many satellites escapes and replacing it with humility's reality and peace,

Humility

Humility is natural, and pride is not. This means that the word *humility* does not define something that's there but something that's not there, and that is pride. However pride is very much there right now, along with arrogance and greed. So the definition of humility is simply pride's absence. Like love, humility brings us together to be where we ought to be, and once again, humility is our natural state of being, while pride is a sick, perverted add-on emotion.

Think about it. All beings are interconnected parts of the gigantic whole (which we might call "the cosmos", except that it's probably much more than that. This means that for us to always be thinking about ourselves alone, makes no sense at all. Plants grow through photosynthesis and reproduce, and animals are guided by their instincts to live, love and reproduce. That's who they are and they do it very well. However we're different because we have the ability to reflect, which should mean that we analyze, reason, think for ourselves and make choices. It certainly means that more than any of the other life forms on the Earth's, we should be aware of just how minute we are, and also be aware of our vast limitations. At the very least we should be aware that we're a part of the Earth's interconnected ecosystems and a part of an interconnected solar system, galaxy, and cosmos. We should be aware of how dependent we are...on the Earth's ecosystems and on everything.

Also in our reflection, we should have long ago concluded that pride, (which makes us believe that we are the most important thing in the cosmos) is not just unnatural, but is just plain stupid. We should also realize that pride is not acceptable, or even decent, because pride and greed are destroying us and most of the life forms on this planet. Pride is a separating, mutant, unhealthy emotion that we have embraced to run wild with our lives, Let me say again, humility is where pride and greed are *not*...where pride doesn't control us or even exist in us. Humility is where, if pride didn't exist in our thoughts and actions, we could live normal, fulfilled, sustainable lives. Pride, unlike The Way with its humility, has absolutely no grounding in the cosmos. It doesn't have the positive, uniting force of the humility in The Way. In fact pride is not connected to anything since it is only a divisive, violent, irrational emotion existing in us to destroy us. .

If we could enter The Way to throw off this parasite to live in humility, our lives would be filled with peace, and our future would be bright. Natural, secure, sustainable humility would replace unnatural, threatening, destructive pride to save us. I'm convinced that no reflective species in the cosmos that ignores The Way to live in pride as we have done, will be able to survive. Any viable evolution must be humbly moving together to be a lasting part of cosmic evolution.

To be humble is to be able to come out of ourselves to look around and see what's there. It is to throw off the illusion that we are *better* than other people, other groups (nations, religions, sexes, races), or other species on this or any planet. Humility brings us out of ourselves so we can see that we are interconnected to and dependent upon everything. Humility underlies The Way, and it's where every reflective life form must be.

I have referred to the *peace* of humility. Most people assume (if they ever think about humility at all) that humility is some kind of religious thing. That's because peace can come from the humility of bowing before some perceived higher power. Doing this can give us some perspective to realize just how small and vulnerable we are. In other words, some religious practices can temporarily alter pride enough to allow people to touch humility. I have seen and known some deeply religious people who I think have found the peace of humility. Most of them have made a retreat from the world in order to be with others who shared this peace. I have always found them to be impressive and inspiring.

However there is a problem in this approach for me, because I don't believe in any of the anthropomorphic god-figures that these people bow before and worship. I am not impressed by superstitions of any kind, so I can't honestly be a part of this. However, as I've studied more and more about the cosmos, I've found the cosmos (which is real) to be impressive and amazing just as these various divine beings, and is also how we were created and came to be. Thus before the cosmos, I often feel the same sense of awe, the same wonder, and the same humility that these religious people feel. In fact the awe that I've felt for life, the Earth and the cosmos were responsible for inspiring me to struggle with being able to write books about humility and The Way.

Being humble results in any number of things. It frees us from our slavery to pride with its demons of hate, violence, worry, and the fear of being ourselves and being real. It can also lead us away from this blind alley into a bright future of unity and peace. This peace that comes from humble living (where we give up trying to control everything and everyone) has been powerful for me and many others.

Also being humble alters how we see ourselves. It can release us from the lie that we are the most important being anywhere or a part of the most important species. It can help us to honestly see how small we are in the world, solar system, galaxy and cosmos. As is taught in many Eastern religions, it can help us to get out of the myth of "self", to see ourselves as "The Whole", as we recognize that we are one with everything in the cosmos.

From all of this I can say to you that there's no question that humility is a basic, necessary path to The Way. It is necessary if we're to enter The Way and have any hope for a meaningful life.

Love

As I've said, love leads us to humility, and humility leads us to love, however love is a bit different from humility. I believe that love differs because it is the powerful, unifying force of The Way that is bringing all units of consciousness together throughout the cosmos. Love is pivotal to The Way not just because it brings people together, but because it is the underlying director ringing *all* cosmic evolution together. Love is the word we have given to this basic force as we have all experienced it. It's much like gravity in matter, as we feel it pulling us and all consciousness (which I believe is in everything) together. Thus this force we call love is a necessary, vital part of evolution's advance. When it is ignored or cast aside by reflective beings, disunity and chaos erupts to hamper and stall their evolution's advance. The insanity we are involved in now in our pride, arrogance, greed, violence and war exemplify that fact. We are choosing the cancerous, renegade emotion of pride over the natural, real, uniting force in the cosmos we've named "love". As I said, we've named it because we know it from being gently touched by its constant, persistent attraction that nudges us together.

Love is revered everywhere. It is the subject, and even core of religions as well as much philosophy, poetry, fiction, and nonfiction. It is the inspiration of ethics and morality, and it is important in such things as law, medicine, and other things where justice and the common good are served. It's a natural, powerful, consistent force that is a vital part of The Way.

The Greeks had three different words for love: **Eros** meaning sexual love, **Philia** meaning family or friendship love, and **Agape** (generally reserved for the gods) meaning an unselfish, unconditional love that includes everyone and everything. Agape love is really what The Way is all about, since it clearly involves loving every person on the Earth and all of it's many life forms. Thus love is deep, far reaching and everywhere. It is a part of everything that is good and is a central part of The Way.

The word love, like the Hebrew word Shalom, is impossible to define. One of the reasons is because its tied to The Way that is embedded within the cosmos that involves everything. Another reason is because love is more wonderful and amazing than we could ever hope to imagine, much less explain. However, as happened with humility, we have tragically evolved away from love and its uniting power. We've evolved so far away that we often can't even feel it anymore. As a reflective species that has embraced pride with it's sick consequences, we have thrown love out....and of course we have simultaneously thrown out The Way. Thus we now blandly accept cruel and unloving things like wealth inequality, militaristic cultures breeding war, the abuse of women and children, gross overpopulation, massive pollution, and the destruction of the Earth's ecosystems.

As reflective beings, we should have long ago evolved together to grow in love. We should be practicing and enthusiastically rejoicing in it. Clearly in our ignorance and abuse of the great force of love, we are betraying the cosmos and our mother Earth (that has birthed us and our brother and sister species). We've chosen the selfish separation of pride's hate, division, fear and prejudice over love's warm, inclusive unity.

Every religion has identified pride as the greatest evil. It is seen in Christianity as one of the seven deadly sins, and at one time it was seen as the foundation of them all. However in the same way, all religions have embraced humility as fundamental to our lives. Both of them are strongly encouraged in all religions and seen as necessary in all beings of common sense, wisdom and goodwill. Thus for all these reason, I believe that love and humility must be the foundation and starting point in our understanding The Way. This love, that's in everything, has sometimes been identified as being divine. It is far more and nothing like the passing emotion of pride, because it's pivotal to life and a vital, necessary part of all beings. Love and humility are so basic to The Way that I believe that without them The Way could not exist.

Of course we could talk about this for the rest of the book, but we need to continue to look at all of the other wonderful word-paths to The Way. All of these path-words demonstrate the great cosmic web of interconnection that is directed by The Way to allow all things to move together and offer us as reflective beings productive, meaningful, evolving lives.

Compassion

Compassion is another important word-path, and If we had evolved correctly into The Way, no one would have even questioned our natural ability to feel compassion for other humans or life forms. Things like national pride, greed, social prejudice, and war have not only drained away our resources but also our sense of compassion, to leave us separated, isolated and alone. We used to see in the news where people had been in a fire or lost a loved one, or where someone had been in a tragic accident, and, even though we didn't know them, we'd still feel real compassion for them....but not anymore. Now we look at the news and don't care that half of the world is hungry and without health-care, or that a huge and growing part of the world has millions of homeless refugees. It just goes right over us. How can this be? What has caused us to throw out almost all of our compassion to ignore everyone whose not close to us? Of course, there are still some people around who do feel some compassion for others, so there is hope.

I think that compassion comes out of our ability to understand and identify with others. It comes when we see that we're all a part of the same species and also a part of *all* species. However we've apparently lost this obvious aspect of our identity to now have little compassion for anyone except our friends or family or sometimes nationality, because we're totally centered in on ourselves.

It's obvious that if we have any compassion left at all, it's for other reflective humans that are just like us, but compassion should include everyone and everything. As the first reflective beings on this planet, we should have naturally evolved to take care of the plants and animals, as well as the Earth, which births and sustains us. We should be like an older sibling looking out for our younger, less experienced ones. We should feel as much compassion for all of Earth's life forms as we do for our families, because they are relatives too. The highly evolved life forms on the Earth struggle for survival and well-being exactly like we do. With the animals, we forget that they love, have children, raise families, and seek ways to feed their children just like we do. Our arrogant pride has caused us to throw out that reality to feel nothing. We even shoot the animals for sport, raise them in cruel conditions to feed us (called industrial farming), and we think nothing about the fact that our disgusting overpopulation is wiping out everything as we eat more and more animals and deforest more and more land.

There is even a mindset that says that animals are our enemies... that they are evil and always waiting to attack us, so we should wipe them out. I will agree that animals, through our abuse and lack of respect, are threatened by us to occasionally strikeout when we approach them. Animals are not stupid. They have brains and they use them. They know that we're very dangerous, so they try to protect themselves and their families from any further abuse and murder. However we also have pets who are animals, who for generations have been protected and even loved by humans. Thus they don't feel threatened, and are very friendly. I would contend that if we left animals alone to live and prosper on their own here beside us, all of the animals would be friendly. We are the reason animals are called "wild", which is a term we use to describe their natural fear of us. Clearly their being dangerous or wild has nothing to do with the animals and everything to do with us!

There are numerous books and documentaries about how far birds, fish, butterflies, caribou, gazelles, zebras and whales migrate each year. Others are about how dolphins, chimpanzees, apes, bears and pigs are very smart. Still others are about how beautiful polar-bears, cheetahs, lions, deer, flamingos and many more are. This line of thought could go on, but the point is that animals are amazing creatures that are a lot like us (or, in our demented state, a lot better). Just as compassion should not be confined to those who are within our families, communities or nation, so our compassion must not leave out the Earth's many species. We are mammals denying that we're animals...which is a catchy phrase that means we're animals too. We are a reflective, animal species, so shouldn't we feel compassion for all of our evolving kinfolk on the Earth as well? And if we did have compassion for them, our actions toward them would have to change...and their response would be to change as well.

We should also feel compassion for what used to be the abundant vegetation on the Earth. Plants are also an advanced life form that grows from their seeds to survive and reproduce in amazing ways, Like us they are very much alive as they take in the carbon monoxide that we breathe out, and releases the oxygen we breathe in. This makes them a valuable part of the Earth's ecosystems as they allow us, and other oxygen dependent animals, to exist.

Big money, big business interests, and the gigantic military/industrial complex think nothing of damaging and destroying nature. Thus they try to brainwash us by calling anyone's compassion for other life-forms degrading things like "tree huger" or "environmental terrorists". They accuse us of wanting to destroy jobs and wreck the economy. Well, I am proud to be a tree huger who stands against the murder of plants and animals, as well as the Earth's ecosystems. I also know that historically jobs and the economy adjust quickly to needed change, and if we stopped abusing plants and animals, we would make that change. However until we can halt run-away greed, we'll continue to feel no compassion for plants or animals to push us off the slippery slope of extinction.

Having compassion for the animals and plants must return whatever the cost,\ or we're out of here...and should be. Of course when we're gone, the Earth will quickly refurbish itself, and possibly even evolve another reflective species. Hopefully that species will *not* be ruled by pride and greed to have compassion for the plants, animals and all life forms, and follow The Way to a sustainable life of peace and joy.

Kindness and Gentleness

Let's talk for a minute about *kindness*. Kindness and love are so intertwined that many feel they're the same thing. Of course kindness is not as important as love since love brings all things together. Still kindness is wonderful thing, and I feel it's clearly a pathway to The Way.

Kindness is a beautiful thing that warms us as we mention it. We've all known kind people who make us smile to think about them. They are people who, even in this world so awash in pride, are able to get out of themselves enough to see and touch our lives with tenderness and care. Kind people rise above their own pain and problems to reach out to others and share their pains and problems. I suspect that somehow, through the miracle of love, they've vaulted over the accepted bitterness and hate that this abused world teaches. They're able to actually feel with and for others to unselfishly approach them. I have often been told the insensitive phrase, "The poor will always be with you". Unless we can appreciate and follow The Way to be kind, this nasty, unkind statement will always be with us too. However I'm also sure that some kind people will always be with us, so we can still have hope for the ending of poverty and the defeat of hate!

One example I've used to help us to identify kindness comes from my years of counseling with people. Married couples who, in growing older, lose the erotic side of the relationship and end up blaming each other to fight all the time. This is actually quite common, but it's not something that has to happen. Some marriages mellow in old age into a pleasant and peaceful relationship, and I think the reason for this is the presence of kindness. I'll admit that some kindness was probably already a part of their relationship, but the fact that it was able to continue into their old age to keep them communicating, sharing, and happy is wonderful. I would often say to a young person getting married, who would ask me what kind of person they should marry, that thinking they were sexy is OK, but if they want to have a long and happy marriage, they need someone who is kind...and then be kind to them.

I think that to be kind is to be *decent* (I love the word decent). It began as a word for a standard of propriety that was accepted by the upper class, but it soon evolved to have a moral side. Now it just indicates what is acceptable and good. It's the appropriate thing to do, and I believe it's most appropriate to be kind. I believe that kindness is not just decent, but it's pleasant, honest and real. It certainly helps us to discern The Way, because The Way is the most kind and decent thing there is.

Associated with kindness, patience and decency is the word *gentleness*. It too originated from a description of the men of the gentry (who were referred to as gentile or gentleman), however now the word has evolved to be seen as a considerate, humble person who treats other people in a caring way. I believe that being gentle, rather than rough with people, is another indication of The Way's presence. People are complicated and delicate beings, and if we can cast aside the pride and ego that makes us compete with and judge everybody, we can see the need to be patient and gentle with them. However society seems to affirm and admire those who are self-centered, pushy, insulting, and rough. As is true of many of the word-paths to The Way, being gentle is generally not admired at all. Still, you have to admit that being around them is a relief. Gentle people are the ones in whose presence I feel most relaxed and comfortable. They are people we don't have to be careful around because we know they won't respond to something we say with ridicule or cruelty. They're people we can trust to be who they appear to be, and that is no small thing.

Sympathy and Empathy

Sympathy is defined as "an affinity or association with someone, so that whatever affects one also effects the other", or "The inclination to think or feel alike". I would just say again that it's the ability to get out of ourselves enough to see who and where people are. It's to feel their pain or fear to enter in and care for them. Like love and all of the word-paths, sympathy brings us together to advance relationships.

Humility and love can sometimes break through to free us enough to feel sympathy. This can come from a lot of things like when we see that someone is facing he same thing that has happened to us, or when our own walls and defenses have fallen enough to allow someone else to help us. However most of the time it just comes from being able to love. When we actually love a partner, a parent, a child, or a pet, sympathy is easy. These are the times when tenderness and trust override our suspicions and fears to allow us to see and truly identify with another person.

Empathy is seen by most of us just to be another word for sympathy. In the dictionary it's defined as "The imaginative projection of one into another, so that the one appears to be infused with the other". To me this is like the old saying, "walk a mile in my shoes". Sometimes sympathy has been seen to be condescending such as doing good in order to appear to be good, but "empathy" is actually entering into the feelings and emotions of others to become them.

I would say that whether you call it sympathy or empathy, it's still a word-path to The Way that brings us together and deserves our attention. Of course if we weren't so sunk in pride, sympathy and empathy would be natural. Identifying with and feeling for other people in their pain or joy, would be the norm.

Forgiveness and Appreciation

Judging is a terrible thing that is condemned in all of the world religions. When we judge, in our superiority we pridefully put ourselves over another person without even having enough evidence to make a decision. It really is a stupid, destructive, disconnecting thing that comes straight out of arrogance.

Forgiveness, on the other hand (which could be said to be the opposite of judging) comes from humility. It is a connecting thing that keeps relationships going rather than destroying them. Of course if we live in pride, it often seems impossible for us to forgive, because pride despises and is the enemy of forgiveness. However there is no doubt that forgiveness is necessary for relationships to survive and one of the path-words to The Way.

I have read many books and attended many seminars on forgiveness. Most of them would set out various steps to learn *how to forgive*. Examples of this might be: identifying the original hurt, telling the one who hurt you that they've done so, and then taking steps to let-go of the hurt. Some of these discussion are helpful, but I don't think they solve the problem.

For instance, a good deal of the time, the other person has no idea that they've hurt us. However we are all so full of pride that we take innocent mistakes and obsess about them. We also take things like a persons different culture or personality, or their indifference to us, as personal insults. Then we go off and pout to find some way to insult them. Thus starts an unnecessary and divisive vicious-circle of animosity. But, of course, even in instances where someone actually meant to be spiteful, we must find a way to get over it for the sake of our mental health. Remember we live in a world that is packed full of animosity and confrontation, so we don't want to just add more! I have often said that in this world so full of pride and arrogance, there can be no community at all unless there's a large dose of forgiveness mixed in. If we left out forgiveness in this chaotic mess, we would end up discarding everybody…and some people do that.

Also, for some people when something is over, it's just over. However, for many of us, everything just hangs on and on. We hold onto not only the anger resulting from people's insults, abuse, or violence; we hang onto everything. We're hoarders of stuff, events, memories, outmoded traditions and more. Thus Forgiveness can only happen when we learn to *let go* and allow our evolution to move on. We have to let go of the past (which is gone) and embrace the present (which is real). All religious writings teach that forgiveness is crucial to a meaningful life, but we ignore them. Forgiveness is right up there with love, kindness, and sympathy, because they all share the same base of humility that directs us to The Way.

To help us to forgive (and thus better understand The Way) we also have to be more thankful and *appreciative*. When we don't appreciate other people, we're much less likely to make the effort to forgive. However we also need to appreciate our own lives and all that sustains them, which includes the Earth and cosmos. However pride is diligently robing us of any appreciation and thanksgiving because we say that we've single-handedly earned everything. so we deserve it. This happens because we're so locked-up in ourselves that we can't see reality enough to appreciate or be thankful for anything, because it's all about "me, me, me".

Losing our ability to be thankful and appreciate things is very sad. It not only robs us of what's real; it robs us of relationships. It shuts us off from what other people, nature and the cosmos constantly do for us. It makes us oblivious to the kindness and nurture that's everywhere around us. Even worse, it repels us away from those who are ready to help us right now. I must say that nothing grieves me more than a person who has become so self-centered that they appreciate nothing...when they've become blind to, and separated from, everybody and everything. None of us ever fully appreciate the miracle of life with its consciousness and its contributions and supports. In truth, all of us are unappreciative clods who allow pride to wipe-out our forgiveness, thankfulness and ability to see The Way.

Thankfulness and appreciation are clearly word-paths that bring us together to approach The Way, so they should underlie our every move. Of course this same thing is true for all of the other reflective beings out there in the cosmos. If any of these evolved beings are to be successful in having meaning and knowing joy, they must hold onto or find the ability to be thankful and appreciative to keep us in touch with reality, and also The Way.

The Paths of Sharing and Giving

These two things are different from the others in that they have to do with things that we do, rather than who we are. Also to share is to give and to give is to share. They are both acts of humility and love that contribute to The Way.

Sharing and giving have become more and more rare in the face of our increasing worship of pride and greed. Sharing and giving have nothing in common with pride; in fact, they are one of pride's biggest nightmares since they tend to negate greed. Greed teaches us to keep everything for ourselves, while sharing and giving recognize that we're interconnected, so they teach us to be generous. However greed is so dominate that it has evolved to be something natural to us.

In many ways our society is built on it, and our system of exchange relies on it. The sad truth is that pride and greed have evolved to be who we are.

The Way holds giving and sharing as its standard. Everyone is connected to and dependent upon everybody and everything else, so shouldn't the common good (that which is good for everyone) be our goal? When you really look at it, it's easy to see that anyone who is suffering, hungry, starving, persecuted or dying affects you and me and everyone else. The same is true for the other lifeforms on the Earth who share our interconnected ecosystems. When anything happens to one, it happens to all. When we look at it this way, you can see how our species pride is driving plants and animals into extinction, however we don't see that we are driving ourselves into extinction as well. The truth is that our species will not be around much longer, and its tragically clear that we are what's doing this.

So of course The Way embraces connectedness and common sense of giving and sharing because this is a necessary part of a healthy reflective species. In other words, unless we recognize our interconnectedness and start evolving together (which is how the cosmos has evolved), our future is a disaster. Giving and sharing are natural and necessary for us. They should be what we are doing without thinking. (Of course everything about The Way is like that, because The Way is also natural...and real.)

Peace

Love for everyone in the world is what can bring about world peace. It cab bring us peace within and peace without. Also justice and peace go together; in fact they're the same thing. To love and work for justice, is to love and work for peace, and visa versa.

Everybody *talks* about "peace", but, since peace has to do with caring for other people (rather than just ourselves), we do nothing about it. We really don't, because all we're concerned about is "me, myself, and I". We're concerned about keeping our delusions of power and control (pride). Each one of us wants to be the best known, most popular, wealthiest, and most dominant person in the world, and the same is true for "my" nation. We want to fulfill all of our ridiculous illusions of superiority, that only lead us to competition, fighting and war and have absolutely nothing to do with peace. We are stuck in confrontation and power that only lead us to more division, violence and war.

When we talk about peace within or peace without, we find that both of them are hard to talk about because they're both so rare. Few of us have ever known any peace within or without because were too busy with our personal, group, and species pride.

Inner Peace

As I said, we have no peace within because we're always trying to do things like pleasing society's demands for what we call "success", meeting the dictates of our parents, or pleasing other people's (or our own) ego. I love the saying,"When you get there where will you be?" We're always blindly pushing ourselves onward into meaningless stress and loneliness where we're awash in fears of failure, bankruptcy or some unidentified personal doom.

Some people attempt to calm these internal storms through their religious superstitions, while others focus on meditation and tradition. I myself have become fascinated with some of the monastic orders that I've visited all over the world. Almost all religions have some form of this. Apparently they exist as an attempt to reach the divine, purify the mind, and find inner-peace. They often accomplish this peace through constantly repeated prayers (such as the Jesus Prayer in Christianity: "Jesus, son of God, have mercy on me"), or meditations using mantras like the holy "Om". These prayers and mantras are done over and over to calm the mind and try to reach divine blessing. In all of the monastic orders that I have visited, they seem to have found a greater degree of inner peace than I've seen anywhere else. (In some cases I also witnessed them as being close to following The Way.) There are also books everywhere that claim to have found ways to reach inner peace. Many no doubt have helped people, but I've found that the relief gained from these things is only temporary. Soon we drift back into our deviate evolution into pride to return to our mental confusion and despair.

In my book on the peace of humility, I point out that if we could live humbly, it really would help us to relieve our various wars within, because most of our mental tumult comes from pride's sick, absurd counsel. Humility could take us out of this self-imprisonment to look around and respond truthfully to what's real.

Of curse for us to be humble, we'd have to make some major changes which I believe can only be achieved by entering The Way (of which humility is a part). The Way offers us the power to lift ourselves out of ourselves to interconnect with everything. The Way can help us to grow up and become who we really are as a part of the evolving cosmos. In other words, when we follow The Way we become who we as reflective beings are supposed to be...real. Remember The Way is real and pride is not, so when we enter it, we become real. To be real is to see ourselves as connected to everything and humbly evolving into the cosmos. We aren't doing that now because our unsettled lives are packed full of fear, worry, guilt, anger, comparisons, competition, violence, war, and prejudice. Thus we live blind to humility, love, kindness, equality (with humans and other species) and peace. Think about it, what could be greater than to know inner peace? As I said, I believe that only The Way, with its humility and love, can get us there.

Outer Peace

Peace without (the peace in communities, nations and the world) can only evolve when love and justice grow enough in us to allow us to get out of ourselves and care for everybody and everything. Peace in the world will come when the sacredness of everyone and all species everywhere, is recognized and affirmed. I have found that outward peace is the reward of loving and the gift of justice. If we had naturally evolved into humility as we followed The Way (instead of the impostor called pride), we would have long ago known peace without. It would be naturally who we are. However as of now our only acquaintance the divisive anger, fear, hate and violence of pride.

However we do yearn – oh how we do yearn – for world peace!

The question is can world peace ever be realized for us, and if so, how? I believe that our greatest block to this is the accepted belief in the sovereignty of nations that is sacred and can't possibly be altered. All nations insist on hiding behind their non-existent borders to build more walls with more weapons to defend themselves. World peace will only come when we can get past this irrational, prideful insistence on "national sovereignty" to find ways to accept, embrace and fully support a world, democratic, representative government of all nations that makes international laws and enforces them. All the nations of the world would unite in a *real* United Nations of the World (much like the United States of America). Then and only then will world peace become a reality.

The time should be ripe for us to accomplish this, because we've now almost evolved out of a time when most of the world's nations were taken over and ruled by foreign powers. When these nations have evolved to be self-ruling and free, they've responded with a period of democratic nationalism. However now we should move past that to form a world, representative, democratic government that can relieve the unbearable weight of military spending and bring real world peace. However it's obvious that we're not even close to doing that because pride's paranoia rules us, and also recently because of the world wide epidemic of terrorism. This is thought to have only come from the Middle East (after the West invaded Afghanistan and Iraq), but in reality most of it is coming from local terrorists. Many nations have turned back to elect far-right candidates to office who are simpleminded, mean, and violent. They are devolving the nations away from The Way that is trying to bring them together.

What we now call the United Nations is devoid of any real power because the Security Council, where the members from the most powerful countries can veto any decision the majority makes (which means it's not a democratic body), is what holds the real power. Also the U.N. has been, and will continue to be, poorly supported. Granted, it's an extremely important and valuable meeting place for needed national discussions, and it serves as the center for multiple humanitarian enterprises which are vital to all nations, but there's no way that anything it decides can be enforced.

Thus when it comes to real peace in the world, very little can now be done. Curbing prideful aggression and war around the world can only be accomplished if the sovereignty of a democratic world government replaces the self-centered sovereignty of individual nations. Only then will world peace, and the end of nuclear threats, be real ...and it's long overdue. Obviously a dramatic move toward humility, unity, and forgiveness (all of which make up The Way) is crucial if we are to ever move to outward peace.

Justice and Unity

Justice and peace would be a good description of The Way if you're asked to give a very short answer. Justice is about the unity and well-being of everything, as The Way is about bringing *all* consciousness into a unified, peaceful whole throughout the cosmos. If justice is present in us, then unity and peace cannot be far behind. You can't have lasting peace or unity without having justice, so we could say that *justice is the foundation of a lasting peace.*

You also can't have justice if you don't first have love, because *justice is love applied to everybody.* Justice comes when we come out of pride's focus on the self to be humble enough to see that we are all equal to each other (as well all other species in the cosmos). Justice is when pride is released from us enough to allow us see that we are all one. (I have often made this point by taking a globe of the Earth and asking people what they saw. Most of them immediately said they saw all of the nations of the world. None of them said that saw that it was *one* world.) All of us on the Earth are the same because we all need food, shelter, community, opportunity and love. It's only when we loose ourselves enough to start yearning and working for *everyone's* well being that we can call ourselves "just". Thus justice is the result of being concerned for everybody, even though we've never seen or known them. Justice is recognizing that we are all citizens of the same world, and then acting on it.

Unity comes from the verb "unite", which means "coming together". I have said over and over that the cosmos evolves as things come together to be more complex than they were before. I believe that this paints a picture of The Way, because with its dominance of humility and love, it bring us together. It unites us with each other, other species, the Earth and the cosmos. It brings us the unity that brings both justice and inner and outer peace. In the cosmos, unless we're moving together we're moving apart; and unless we're uniting we're falling apart. Thus that's what The Way does: it unites us and brings justice to us...it opens us up to moving together to evolve into the cosmos.

Unity shows us the truth that we are actually one. We are all one unified species that is a part of one world, one solar-system, one galaxy and one cosmos. Everything about us is tied to everything else, so we actually *are* everything else! We are the Earth and we are cosmic dust. Until we can fathom this from knowing The Way, we will remain disunited, confused, miserable, fighting and temporary. We will continue to evolve into even more fear, anger, worry and guilt. We will miss the vision of peace and seeing that we are a part of everything in the evolving, amazing Earth and the powerful, endless cosmos. One of the most wonderful realities that The Way teaches is that everything, including all of us, make up one mighty, united cosmos.

Thus justice and unity are an important part of The Way, and by following The Way, we will meet them. (They can also be found in some religions and philosophies that have picked up on The Way.)) However things like revengeful punishments (including capital punishment), greed in government and business, available guns, militaristic societies, the abuse of women and children, our frequently recurring wars, and our abuse of the Earth continue to demonstrate that we now have no interest in justice or unity, which means that we have not interest in The Way...but we still struggle onward grasping for hope and anticipating a better day.

Equality, Freedom, and Egalitarianism

The concept of *Equality* has been around for ages, but it hasn't been taken seriously so hasn't been accomplished. Social inequality goes back to when pride began. Inequality seems to have exploded at the end of our nomadic lifestyle in the formation of large groups to farm and domesticate animals. Then they developed armies to defend "their" space, and they switched from worshiping the Earth to worshiping the sky. Dictatorial figures and holy men evolved to receive greater and greater respect.

Soon land "ownership" by individuals (which is a silly concept) emerged to give those who supposedly owned the land great power over those who were just on the land who had no power at all. They were called "serfs" who labored for the landowners just to survive. Soon military leaders defending large city-states grew in power to be named "kings" who ruled over everybody. As cities grew, builders and artisans of various kinds emerged who were also honored and respected.

The concept of wealth ultimately brought forth the concept of "money" which altered everything. A horrific cast system evolved as an accepted part of the society and even a part of their religions. Eventually the myths that kings and queens had divine rights appeared, followed by their royal courts with designated nobles. Such kings, through war and conquest, grew to rule over several territories, and through more violence, they got even more. Thus war, violence, conquest, and cruel control over vast empires became the norm. Any thought of equality was totally lost and replaced by a nonsensical, unjust inequality. This not only became accepted, but it was the only thing anyone expected or even wanted..

This prideful concept of equality, that pretends that a few are better than all the rest, is still totally accepted. Over the years, the word "*freedom*" did grow to express a growing awareness of inequality. Freedom means the absence of tyranny and dictatorial control (and sometimes being free of one group controlling another), and it is still growing all over the world. This freedom is now why so many revolutions are taking place in the world. Examples in the past are the French revolution (which ended in chaos with Napoleon), the American (USA) revolution (that started a worldwide move to representative democracy) and the Russian and Chinese revolutions (that espoused Communism). All of these revolutions were seeking some form of equality, and they all initially claimed to have achieved it, even though none of them really did. The rule of pride is so basic to us and our societies, that real equality is still just a dream.

Freedom and equality are often mentioned by the world's religions. What has been called "the all-inclusive way" was basic to the original teachings of Buddhism, Christianity, Taoism and many others. Of course myths and superstitions overshadowed those early enlightened teachings to leave them now only occasionally mentioned. Still in our time, enlightened people like Mahatma Gandhi, Martin Luther King, Nelson Mandela, and others have known and worked for these obvious truths in practical ways that have benefited us all.

Egalitarianism, which is much like equality, is a word that means treating everyone and everything the same and with equal respect, appreciation and love, because all life forms deserves it, since all of us are miraculously alive, and are one. Egalitarianism not only refers to the fact that everything is connected to everything else, but that everything actually *is* everything else that makes up the interconnected web we call the cosmos. I believe that if we could understand this and internalize it, we would be egalitarian. Once again, to be egalitarian means to be all-inclusive of *all* people (both individuals and groups), *all* species, *all* of the Earth, the solar systems, and galaxies of the cosmos. Of course it also includes treating *all* nationalities and *all* religions exactly the same.

If we were following The Way, being all-inclusive would be natural, and if we were all-inclusive we would be naturally following The Way. Being all-inclusive is what's real for us so it's what we must be. It's a part of The Way that has to be a part all reflective beings throughout the evolving cosmos to survive. Each of us must find our path to egalitarianism, instead of continually evolving into pride's exclusiveness.

Democracy

Democracy is a word-path to The Way that most people think they know everything about, but actually democracy is a very complicated, complex subject. You may think it's strange to mention it in our discussion of the paths to The Way because it refers to an evolved political system of governing. However it does stand against tyranny and dictators that come out of pride/control. It also should stand for governments that justly uphold freedom and equality for everyone and give everyone a voice in their governing, because democracy is meant to be be government "of the people, by the people, and *for the people"*.

Democracy's evolution is a complicated one. It was first recorded in Athens Greece before 500 BC where it was tried by several different tribes and groups. We can also find experiments of it in Sparta, Mesopotamia, India, and of course Rome. Other early places might be medieval England, Scotland, the Isle of Man, Iceland, Ireland and Italy. There is some evidence that indigenous people, such as the American Indians, gave it a try.

In the modern era we find democracy springing up in Poland, the Virginia House of Burgess-es, the Mayflower Compact, the English Petition of Rights, William Penn in Pennsylvania, and the 1689 Bill of Rights in England. In 1776 we see it in the Virginia Declaration of rights followed by the famous writing of the US Constitution. In 1791 democracy continues to bloom in the US Bill of Rights and the 1799 French and Haitian revolutions.

There were waves of democracies that arrived after the end of the European empires, and also after the First World War. Numerous civil rights movements also resulted from this, and many others came after World War II. There were also democratic waves after the end of the Cold War in places like Russia and China's provinces. Quite recently, we have witnessed democratic revolutions in nineteen countries including Tunisia, Egypt, Libya, Yemen, Bahrain, Algeria and Syria that's been called the "Arab Spring".

After the shocking loss of life in both the First and Second World Wars, there were attempts to form a representative, democratic, world governance (much like the United States with its various States) to stop the nations from fighting future wars. Both attempts (The League of Nations and The United Nations) have done a lot of good in providing a forum for discussions and crucially important joint humanitarian actions. However because the UN's enforcement body is its Security Counsel where powerful nations can veto any action taken, and also because national sovereignty remains dominant in the world, the UN has always been underfunded and unable to stop most wars. It's clear to me that unless we can find some way to have a *real* world, democratic, representative government, the insanity and loss of war will continue to plague us, and even destroy us.

We must also admit that our so-called democracies still have serious problems. Thus the long evolution of democracy is far from over, and in many ways, it has just begun. What is called the democratic rule often comes down to the rule of the rich and powerful, or the military and big business. Democracies also suffer from lethargic, uneducated, uninformed voters. Needless to say we have a long way to go before we can witness a pure democratic system that is unaffected by the special interests and big money that reflect our individual, group and species pride.

Another problem is biased voting laws (that limit the ability of certain people to vote), and also poor, inadequate, and out of date voting procedures. Cheating by political parties or powerful individuals that don't follow voting rules is so common that many elections around the world have to be monitored. It's not unusual for an election needing to be taken over. Until a respect for, and the recognition of, the fact that the right to vote is the fuel that keeps a democracy going, and democracy itself is seen as being more important than the power and greed that often wins elections, the problems of inequality in week democratic systems will endure.

Which brings us to why I feel that democracy is one of the paths to the Way. I have often said that it's a miracle that any democracy at all has been able to evolve in our pride engulfed societies, I think that democracies emerge out of our commonsense, justice and humility that comes from The Way's continued presence within us.. Democracy brings people together to seek the common good over the self-interest of the few. It recognizes that we are all interconnected so, the health and well-being of one is the health and well-being of all.

When the value of democracy is fully recognized on every level, it is a magnificent avenue to peace and justice. I say "recognized on every level" because some very misguided people or nations have tried to *force* democracy on others who have no education, background or appreciation of its worth, and that has had led to tragic results. A tyrannical approach to something that stands against tyranny is ridiculous. Of course much of the time the claims that "our nation is responsible for bringing democracy to other nations" is just an excuse to take over and advance a nation's self-interest in things like oil, military bases, or even territorial advancement.

But none of this can ever detract from democracy's great value and what it has done for us. It is a light in the national darkness of greed's injustice, and I believe that it is intimately associated with The Way.

Intimacy

The word intimacy describes a relationship that is very close, loving and trusting. Of course the word "intimacy" is often used to describe sexual relationships, but in our prideful society, much of the time even that is not so. Sex does not always produce intimacy, but if the intimacy is already there, sex can enhance intimacy. This simply means that two or more people are connecting with each other in a deep, meaningful and compassionate way, whether sex is involved or not. Because of sexual abuse, many believe that most intimacy is found in other relationships like families, friendships, group gatherings or other acquaintances.

Intimacy is definitely associated with families and close friends, because, in a prideful society, it's extremely hard for people to develop any relationships at all. Of course even family relationships can be difficult. All of our relationship are hindered by our lack of humility and trust that leaves us frustrated, angry, and verbally (or even physically) abusive. It's a vicious circle of anger or abuse as we respond with more anger or abuse to wound and scar our relationships.

We all walk around with these emotional scars, but some of us are so wounded that we can't trust intimacy at all. Many others who are hurt still try to move together anyway, to end up just faking intimacy. This ends in large numbers of miserable, broken relationship that then encourages their lack of trust to gives them even more scars. Pride in its separation teaches us to hate and annihilate our intimacies. It drives us apart, and pushes us further into our already miserable selves.

Of course all of this is why intimacy is so rare. However it's also why it is so cherished when can be found. If everyone could humbly live in The Way, *all* of our relationships would be healthy ones that allowed us to testify to the beauty and peace of real intimacy. Clearly Intimacy is a word-path of The Way.

There are so many more things that might be mentioned in a list of word-paths, however I hope that I've given you enough of them to make you see that something...some power that is out there, around us, and within us...is crucial to our evolution both now and into the future. Only by living within The Way of ;the cosmos will we ever really know what the words joy, security, peace and intimacy mean, and only by embracing The Way can we find a future for our species. The value and presence of The Way (which I hope you're beginning to see) is far beyond our silly words or imaginings not only because we have tried avoid it, but also because The Way, as a part of the cosmos, is mystically evolving to bring us and everything together everywhere.

We join spokes together in a wheel,
but it is the center hole
that makes the wagon move.
We shape clay into a pot,
but it is the emptiness inside
that holds whatever we want.
We hammer wood for a house,
but it is the inner space
that makes it livable. Tao te Ching

V Things that Help Us Recognize The Way

I came to see The Way through my own personal evolution, and each of us must do the same. We must come to recognize it out of our own, unique experiences. However I believe that even though The Way is now difficult for us to understand, there are some things common to us all that can help us to recognize the The Way. Of course, I am biased in this discussion because of my specific evolution, but I'll still offer a few suggestions anyway.

Religions

You may remember that I said that the study of world religions was very helpful to me in being able to see and approach The Way. This is because most religions have had founders and early followers who were aware of The Way and enthusiastically taught it. That"s why I've said that the majority of religions in the world still have The Way at their base. We can clearly see this in their teachings on humility, love, giving, sharing, justice, peace, forgiveness and many other things that bring us together. This means that The Way clearly touched and directed all of the world's religions in the past and even now. Right now there are many people in all of the word religions who teach and attempt to follow these teachings that reflect The Way. Of course the credit for the existence of teachings is generally ascribed to the various religion's gods or spirits, but it is abundantly clear to me that The Way of the the cosmos in nature and each one of us is what has inspired these these teachings. However whatever you may say about how these ideas and teachings came to be even in the face of our sick pride, the fact is they are here now. Thus even today The Way is present in all of the world's religions, and now I can see how it has greatly affected my life as well as millions of others. It's because of this that I am beginning this section with the subject of religions. I no longer follow or belong to any one religion because now having studied them all, I find that I appreciate all of them as they struggle for meaning, truth, direction and truth in this species sad and precarious environment.

Please understand from what I've just said that I could never be *against* any religion when they are a major purveyor of The Way. I see The Way as what is supplying the ethical and moral glue that is holding our violent, disconnected world together. Without The Way and with it being in all religions, we would be in a much worse mess. I've also come to see a difference between silly superstitions and wise, time-tested myths. I believe that many *myths* are really beliefs that are a part of our history teaching us deep truths that should be preserved. Many myths have incredible stories to tell us that offer us understanding and wisdom on our journeys. As I've said, nations and religions should not try to be melting-pots that make us all the same, but they would be mixed-salads where all cultures, races, religions, philosophies and backgrounds are welcomed and accepted. This certainly includes the myths of indigenous people such as North and South American Indians, Africans and Australians. We can grow from their teachings and history as we appreciate and conserve them all. It is very important that we never miss any opportunity to row in wisdom, but we should also be careful not to take any myth literally. When we make this mistake, our myths stop teaching us to become agents of superstition, divisiveness, and disconnection that are based on pride.

I think superstitions can halt our moving on in education and evolution. They get us stuck in outmoded ideas and prejudices that have been proven to be wrong. I tend to link pride and superstition together because pride and superstition always try to disrupt our search for truth. They rob us of our interconnectedness and sometimes even our evolution. Many superstitions began with things that were historical, but over time their exaggerations and lies took over to make them silly and dangerous distractions. We must be willing to evolve and move on as we admit that some things are outmoded (even when parents taught them to us). Examples of this are prejudices about race, nationalism, religion, the sexes, where we've been taught that ours is the best and the only one that matters. Such teachings may involve things that have never been up-dated and have become detrimental to our personal evolution.

So where do we go to find the truth of who we are and should be? I used to believed that it emerges each day we test the validity of our actions, but now I know that it can only come as we look to The Way. It is only from the Way that we as prideful creatures that find real morality and truth. That is where we can see what's separating us and what is bringing us together. I find that outmoded superstitious beliefs inspired by pride are one of our worst enemies as they block our ability to see and enter the uniting, healing force of The Way.

I must say again that though I admire and respect all religions, they are still infested with pride and its self-centered, exclusive, greedy, power hungry violence. As I've said, there is a continuing struggle going on in the world's religions right now between those who are instinctively drawn to The Way found within them, and those who have totally lost sight of it in pride. Thus The religions of the world are divided into two groups: those who concentrate on their own selfish superstitions, and those who concentrate on The Way in their religions. As I now look back at my own experience in ministry, I can see how this struggle affected my life, and how it also limits the religion's influence on our societies. All religions teach us about love and do a lot of good. They provide needed community to separated people who are struggling who need it so dearly. However I am against the pride and superstition that so pervade them to make them exclusive, mean, arrogant and at times violent.

Of course religion is not the only thing that has been influenced by The Way (we will discuss some of them later). Thus the concept of God presented in different ways in many religions) is not the only, necessary motivation for experiencing or acting out The Way. This powerful, unifying cosmic ethic is in everything, everywhere. Fortunately some religious people, as they humbly bow before their divine being, have been able reach enough humility to know its peace. However The Way (which begins with humility) cannot ever just be tied to religions. Though it is possible to live an ethical, contributing, loving life as a religious person perceiving the The Way, the same thing happens without any religious commitment by people who are just as humble and loving. The motivation can come from many places. It can come from common-sense observations from of our reflected wisdom because, as I keep saying, The Way exists in and touches everything. It is not necessary to be religious to be ethical, kind, and responsible. I believe the real motivation is the wisdom and desire to be who we are meant to be...real, honest, reflective beings who seek The Way. In my own life's evolution, I've found (and I expect this might also be true for you) that The Way can be seen and discovered by a variety of people in their personal, unique ways, and I find this to be very comforting. Each one of us will find it differently, but each one of us must find it to truly live.

I am always eager, in spite of the pride that has eaten up all of the world's religions, to point out The Way's powerful presence in them. Thus I will offer you a little bit about some of these religions, and suggest a few of their writings that I think indicate the presence of The Way. Of course I can only choose a few, but maybe this taste will stimulate you to study and look for The Way in even more.

(If you want to study the subject of the evolution of religions, and are interested in some of my opinions on the subject of a divine being, you can look at Appendices III.)

Christianity

I'll begin this discussion on world religions with Christianity, because it's the one in which I grew up and then taught for many years, so I obviously know the most about it. Of course my perception of Christianity changed when I started doing research into things like who Jesus really was and when I studied the recently translated scriptures and theological reflections of the other world religions. All of this was very challenging, but I was able to learn, grow and evolve immensely.

What I've discovered from recent discoveries about Jesus is that he was one of the many Jewish prophets of his time who challenged the establishment to be charged with treason. However Jesus was very different from the other prophets of his day in that he never talked about, or had any intention of, leading an insurrection against Rome. However that was still why the Romans had him killed.

Jesus was very popular among the many poor, persecuted, sick and outcast who followed him to form a large community of poor, outcast people out in the wilderness. This community was nonjudgmental and all-inclusive. It took in people of every class as well as outlawed women and men, slaves and the castaway sick. He welcomed people of all faiths including the hated Samaritans and people of all nationalities like Romans and Greeks...and anyone else. He was a Jew, so he preached about Yahweh, but he was different. He said that Yahweh was not a God of punishment and revenge, but a God of love who forgave and appreciated everybody. He accepted Yahweh as the God of everyone who was total compassionate, accepting and peaceful.

Jesus was a humble man who taught humility and love in regard all things. He would never have chosen twelve disciples over the other followers, because he believed in complete egalitarianism where everyone was treated exactly the same. (The disciples in scripture seem to have evolved from leaders in the early church.) He was obviously a powerful charismatic teacher who, in his inclusion of discarded people, not only gave them hope, but for those who had been cast out because of illnesses, his total acceptance allowed them psychologically and physically to improve and even be healed.

His popularity and strange ways threatened the power of both the Jews and Romans who were in wealthy, prideful positions, so when he lost his temper in a Jerusalem synagogue because of their greed, he was condemned by the authorities and executed. His followers went out to carry on his teachings calling them "The Way" (which is what Jesus had called his teachings), and it continued to be used until the slang expression "Christianity" stuck. *(One of my favorite book on the life of Jesus was called Jesus, A Revolutionary*

Biography by John Dominic Crossan, who was one of the founders of the fascinating "Jesus Seminar".)

Needless to say after his death Jesus's teachings quickly began to be compromised as pride and greed crept in. Ever new myths and stories evolved around him to threaten everything he was and taught. For instance, the name " Christ" that was given to him came from a Jewish myth about an anticipated Messiah. This addition said that Jesus was this Messiah (Christ in Greek). Numerous other myths evolved that were accepted within the growing traditions. For instance, myths exploded about his birth and death, and with each passing year, they became more and more imaginative. About fifty years after his death, stories about his life, that were mixed with all of these myths, began to be written down. Each new writing after that was filled with even more of these myths. For instance, Jesus came to be called "The Son of God" who had gone up to heaven to be at the right hand of Yahweh. Myths said that you could pray to Jesus and he would forgive your sins, heal your diseases, and intercede with Yahweh on your behalf. Eventually it was said that if you believed in Jesus, at your death you would go to a beautiful place called "heaven" rather than an ugly place called "hell". Gradually Jesus, who was a very humble man, was turned into a God that was worshiped all over the world.

Eventually what was now called Christianity fell into disfavor with the Romans, and as it separated from Judaism, it faced persecution from both Rome and Judaism. Roman persecution went on until a Roman emperor prayed to Jesus (called "The Christ") in a battle where the emperor was later victorious. Thus he returned to Rome and required the whole Roman Empire to convert to Christianity. He also brought together Christian leaders from all over the empire to form one accepted version of Christian scripture (called The Cannon) and one theology (called the Nicene Creed). Both were an attempt to present a unified picture of what Christians believed.

By this time, nothing but a small remnant of Jesus' original teachings were left hidden in the four accepted writings about Jesus attributed to early church leader's known as Mark, Luke, Matthew and John. This book came to be called "The Bible", and it evolved to be seen as more than just a writing but as something sacred and holy that came straight from God. This book was never to be questioned or altered (though it was edited and changed many times in translation). The Bible soon came to be seen as containing the only truth and became "the rule of faith and practice". The "Church" has continued to grow in pride, power, influence and also in its superstitions and mythology.

As I've said, I would be the first to say that a lot of good has come from Christianity as well as all of the other world religions in things like the comfort of a caring community, encouragement and hope in living, acts of unselfish charity, opportunities for community service, support for schools and hospitals, and of course encouraging compassion, love, forgiveness, peace, honesty, justice, and equality. Missionaries (trying to convert people to their own religion) have done some good, but they've also pushed their own exclusive cultural ideas upon trusting kind people who naturally evolved from other religions and cultures.

As is true of all of the religions that were started by charismatic, very wise leaders, Christianity has had some positive influences on our evolution most ow which came come from Jesus' original teachings. Great arguments will continue about whether or not the religion's positive influences outweigh their negative ones, but I've found that there have been many positive things that have uplifted our species even in the face of pride/control. However we can't ignore the terrible things coming from religious pride that has left the world caught up in wars where millions of people have been killed. Also Christianity's exclusive views, that looks down on others and tries to convert everyone, are horrible. (I have often said that religions are not evil; it's the arrogance and pride in them that's evil).

I will now look at a few of the teachings from the New Testament of Christianity that indicate the original teaching of Jesus and the presence of The Way. Let me say again that such teachings are found in *all* of the world's religions, but each religion claims them to be their own. These teachings are said to *be* Christian, Jewish, Buddhist, Muslim, Taoist or some other religion, when in reality these teachings are in all religions and have come from The Way.

Examples of The Way in Christian Teachings

Though I may speak with the tongues of men and of angels but have not love, I am become as sounding brass or tinkling cymbal. And though I have the gift of prophecy and understand all mysteries and all knowledge, and though I have all faith so I could remove mountains, and still have no love, I am nothing. And though I bestow all my goods to feed the poor and give my body to be burned and have no love, I am nothing. Love suffers long and is kind; love envies not; love vaunts not itself and is not puffed up. It does not behave unseemly, seeks not one's own, is not easily provoked and thinks no evil. I Corinthians 15

The fruit of the spirit is love, joy, peace, long-suffering, gentleness, goodness, faith, meekness, and temperance. Galatians 5

You shall not commit adultery, you shall not kill, you shall not steal, you shall not bear false witness, you shall not covet, and if there are other commandments that are not comprehended in the statement, you shall love your neighbor as yourself. Love works no ill to your neighbor so love is the fulfillment of the law. Romans 1

A new commandment I give to you, that you love one another; as I have loved you, you should also love one another. By this all people will know that you are my followers if you have love one for another. John 13

Do to others as you would have them do to you. Luke 6

Truly I tell you, just as you did not do it to one of the least of these, you did not do it to me. Matthew 25

If anyone strikes you on one cheek, offer the other also. Luke 6

Love you enemies; do good to those who hate you; bless those who curse you; pray for those who abuse you. When anyone takes away your coat, do not withhold even your shirt. Give to everyone who begs from you, and if anyone takes away your goods, do not ask for them back. Luke 6

Put your sword back into its place; for all those who take up the sword will perish by the sword. Matthew 26

Humanity's great wisdom traditions are given not to compete with each other but to complete each other. We need each other as much as the species of the earth need one another to be whole.

Re-birthing will happen within our Christian household when we reverently approach the heart of other traditions. It is what Griffins in his work in India calls the "marriage of East and West," a conjoining of what has been tragically torn apart.

We need to find ways of sharing our intimate experiences of the Mystery, for we are one. It is through one another that we will know more of the Life that flows within us all. It is through sharing our fragments of insight that we will come to a fuller picture of the One who is at the heart of each life.

Too often in the past our approach to truth has been to assume that we have it and others do not. Consequently, we have thought that our role is to tell people what to believe. We are being invited instead into a new humility, to serve the holy wisdom that is already stirring in the hearts of people everywhere, the growing awareness of earth's inter-relatedness and sacredness. John Philip Newell

Other Religions

Obviously I've concluded from my research that all of the world religions are equally valuable and very similar. If you don't like this statement, I can understand because I was not always aware of it either. I was brought up to believe that Christianity was the only religion, and if there were any others, they were just silly and wrong. I was a christian minister for the major part of my life and worked within the Church. I believed in mission work and the passing on of the Gospel (good news) to other cultures.

If there were other religions, I ignored them because I had no time for them, and I was sure they were too far out to even think about. I loved the wisdom, comfort, kindness, and community of the church, and I believed as C. S. Lewis said, "If Christianity isn't true, then it ought to be". I worked so hard that I never took any time to actually study other religions, but when I did, I was amazed. I realized how much I'd missed and how mistaken I'd been. I was able to see that other religions have the same commitment from their followers and the same appreciation of their own religion's wisdom, comfort, kindness and community as I have had. Of course we all come out of different cultures, histories and backgrounds, so we all have differences in our approach, but I've found that our similarities far outweigh these differences...and are really amazing!

I've now been able to clearly see that all religions have the same underlying ethic that I have recently been able to see, and I've called it The Way (which inspired this book). I've already pointed out that The Way has helped me to answer questions like, "Well, what religion are you really?...what do you believe?...what faith do you follow?...who do you think you are?" I can now say that I believe in, and try to follow the cosmic ethic I call The Way which is in all religions....and then I lamely try to explain further.

It is obvious that because each one of the world's religions comes from a different cultural evolution, they all have different views on subjects like life after death, the presence and influence of a divine being, or whether we should have an inner or outer focus in life. Still in spite of this, they are all similar in things like love, compassion, wisdom, and their concern for humble worship, community and ethical, meaningful lives. They may be different, but I believe that even these differences can be instructive and helpful to those who are willing to be open and listen to them.

I guess I've now moved out of my previous religious pride enough to be open to all other religions and be eager to learn from them. In our present slavery to pride, we honestly believe that our religion is the best and *only* one, so being open to other religions is impossible. However we can make the journey to see the obvious common thread that runs through them as they struggle to find meaning, comfort and truth in what I call The Way.

Judaism

Judaism has a lot in common with Christianity because Jesus was a faithful Jew. His goal was to reform Judaism not separate from it. The fact that this separation did occur after his death would have appalled him. After his death, the two religions were so connected that when Christian scripture was formulated into "The Cannon", over half of its writings were taken from Jewish scripture to be what is now called The Old Testament.

Abraham (also claimed by Islam) was the first prominent Jewish leader, but it was around 1285 BC that another well known Jewish leader emerged named Moses. He was able to instill in his enslaved people a sense of unity and identity that centered on a God named Yahweh (there were many Gods at that time). Of course the events of these people's origin were written down much later, and the myths that evolved around them were exaggerated and rewritten over the years. However these events have defined the Jewish people to this day.

However, the Yahweh that Moses worshiped was still not seen as the one and only God immediately, but it was seen as the national God of the newly united Israelite tribes. Thus Moses can be seen as one more step up from Mesopotamian and Egyptian polytheism, but it would still take a long time to reach actual monotheism. We see this subject being addressed in the Jewish prophets, the wisdom literature, and most especially during the Babylonian Exile (that lasted from 587 to 536 B.C).

However so powerfully did the concept of one God in Jewish thought eventually evolve, that when they were taken over by the Greeks, and later the Romans and told to worship their many gods, they refused to give up this central belief. They were adamant that there is only one God whose name is Yahweh (who they eventually believed was the unrecognized God of everyone).

The Tanach and Talmud influences were added to the Torah, and they have all been interpreted in vastly different ways by the various branches of Judaism. From Abraham, to Moses to great prophets like Isaiah, the impact of this small religion has been immense, and remains so to this day.

Examples of The Way in Jewish Teachings

The wolf shall live with the lamb; the leopard shall lie down with the kid; the calf and the lion and the fatling together; and a little child shall lead. The cow and bear shall graze; their young shall lie down together; and the lion shall eat straw like the ox. The nursing child shall play over the hole of the asp, and the weaned child shall put its hand on the adder's den. They will not hurt or destroy on all my holy mountain, for the Earth will be full of the knowledge of the Lord as the waters cover the sea. Isaiah 11

Pride goes before destruction, and a haughty spirit before a fall.

It is better to be of a lowly spirit among the poor than to divide the spoil with the proud. Before destruction, one's heart is haughty, but humility goes before honor.

If your enemies are hungry, give them bread to eat, and if they are thirsty, give them water to drink. Proverbs 16, 18, 25

Seek good and not evil, that you may live; and so the Lord, the God of hosts, will be with you, as you have said. Hate evil and love good and establish justice at the gate; it may be that the Lord, the God of hosts, will be gracious to the remnant of Joseph" (Amos 5:14-15).

How blessed are those who keep justice, who practice righteousness at all times' Psalm 196

He has shown you , O mortal, what is good. And what does the Lord require of you? To act Justly and to love mercy and to walk humbly with your God. Micah 6:8

You shall do no injustice in your judgment; you shall not be partial to the poor nor defer to the great, but you are to judge your neighbor fairly. Leviticus 19

The strength of the King loves justice. You have established equity; You have executed justice and righteousness in Jacob. Psalm 99

Islam

Islam, coming from the word "Salaam" (meaning peace or surrender) emerged in the hot, barren desert of Saudi Arabia in 622 AD to a people whose ancient polytheistic religion was in the process of dying. Their lives had been subject to the fate of desert jinns (spirits), marauding desert Bedouins, the whims of a brutal ruling class, and the exploitation of corrupt merchants. Centuries of contact with Judaism and Christianity in the Near East, Egypt, and

North Africa (which were sometimes friendly and sometimes not), had familiarized them with the concept of one God. However, Islam evolved to be as different from Christianity as Christianity evolved to be different from Judaism. Having said this, I would point out again that they all saw themselves as descendants of Abraham (using much of the same scripture), and Islam believed that both Moses and Jesus were great prophets.

Islam believes that Mohamed was the last and greatest of the prophets. They believe that he brought the message of enlightenment from the Angel Gabriel that's now recorded in the Koran. Out of the peoples polytheistic past, the prophet Mohamed preached of Allah, the one God who spoke to his people through his prophet. He called them to a new way of life and a new way of looking at religion. He too called for them to worship the one God.

Contrary to our knowledge of Jesus, we know that Mohamed was born in 571 AD in Mecca. Both his parents died when he was a child. He was cared for by his grandfather and then by an uncle. He worked as a shepherd and later, as a caravan worker organizing caravan trips. In spite of the horrible corruption and graft around him, he was known as an upright and trustworthy man. At 25, he was hired by a wealthy widow to manage her affairs. Later they were married. She loved and assisted him throughout his life and mission.

Troubled by the horrible conditions around him, Mohamed took time off from his work to live in a cave close to Mecca. There he prayed and ask for solutions to the problems that were destroying his people. Here he developed a relationship with a divine being called Allah, which was the name of one of the many spirits of his countrymen at the time. He became convinced that Allah was neither a spirit nor just another God, but he was the one and only God. Soon the famous phrase, that was to unify and rally a divided and burdened people, rang out through the entire world "La Ilaha Illa Allah!" (There is no God but Allah). Mohamed preached his message to free the people of Mecca from their ignorance, superstition, graft, abuse and bondage to reach immorality.

The myth that grew up after his death says that around this time when he was in the cave a voice came to him three times saying, "recite." Then, the angel Gabriel dictated the Qumran to him. Mohamed spent the rest of his life in an uncompromising and unrelenting effort to bring this message of Allah to his people.

He made it clear that he could work no wonders and was only a preacher. He suffered, as did Moses and Jesus, great persecution, ridicule and humiliation. He was cutting into the revenues paid to the shrines and temples of the many of the spirits by preaching that there was only one God and that all people were equal and should live moral lives. This threatened the rigid social structure, economy, and political order Of Mecca. Also Mohamed's strict moral code threatened the establishment to bring his community even more persecution.

He had to leave Mecca. This "hegira" (flight) in 622 A.D. is the Islamic point for determining dates. After 3 years he had less than 40 followers. However, after 10 years he had won over 5,000 people to his cause. Gradually, not only did he become a preacher, leader, and politician, but persecution forced him in the name of Allah to defend himself and become a warrior. There is no doubt that this changed him, but he insisted that it was only self-defense However upon his death in 632 A.D., essentially all of Arabia was under his control. One hundred years later Muslims, with their 5 principals (or obligations) imposed by the Koran, controlled a large part of the world.

Examples of The Way in Islamic Writings

O you who believe, enter absolutely into peace. Qur'an 2

There is no compulsion where the religion is concerned.

You cannot guide those you would like to, but God guides those that He will. He has best knowledge of the guided. Qur'an 2 and 28

God does not forbid you from being good to those who have not fought you in the religion or driven you from your homes, or from being just towards them. God loves those who are just. Durat al-Mumtahana 8

Guidance is not attained except with knowledge, and correct direction is not attained without patience. Ibn Taymiyah

Stop acting so small. You are the universe in ecstatic motion... What you seek is seeking you.

Your task is not to seek love, but merely to seek and find all the barriers within yourself that you have built against it. Lovers don't finally meet somewhere. They're in each other all along.

You are not a drop in the ocean; you are the entire ocean in a drop. There is a voice that doesn't use words. Listen. Rumi

(There are more Rumi quotes at the conclusion of this book)

Hinduism

Beginning with Hinduism. all eastern religions look for the divine inside of us, while beginning with Judaism, all western religions beginning look for the divine outside of us. Eastern religions see the divine hidden beneath the chaos of our thoughts and feelings, thus it can only be accessed by shutting them all down through meditation. All religion's have some form of meditation, but for Eastern religions it is necessary. I believe that some degree of consciousness can be found in everything, so it constantly flows like a river throughout the cosmos. Thus it may be that if we can calm-down or silence our busy computer minds, we would be able to access this underlying consciousness to experience a sense of oneness, belonging and peace that our minds are shutting out.

Hinduism is by far the oldest religion going back to the early evolution of humanity. The many invasions of **India** served to contribute to the already amazing complexity of the gods in Hinduism. They always had the ability to see the religion of their conquerors as some further expression of their own. Basically, they believe in Brahman the creator, Vishnu the preserver, Shiva the destroyer, but they also accept a huge pantheon of Gods (purported to approach 33 million).

Around these Gods, ancient myths going back to the hunter/ gathers have grown and multiplied. They've been accepted as an imperfect attempt to understand the different aspects of Brahman. Of course, Hinduism, as was true of all religions, was early mired in its own complex cacophony of superstitions with things like spirits, miracles, magic, reincarnation and Karma (that was behind their rigid caste system)

The Hindu concept of person was seen as the expression of a reservoir of being that never dies, an infinite center, a hidden presence that's often referred to as "Atman". He was the world's soul from which all other souls came and to which all souls would return. This hidden center in everything was also seen as being a part of Brahman.

However they believed that instead of identifying with this innermost soul, humans have chosen to identify with a surface-self. Thus to throw off the preoccupation with this illusion to attain union with their deepest divine-self (called Nirvana), Hinduism developed various elaborate systems, or

Paths to approach Nirvana.

They also developed a strong belief in reincarnation and Karma. This meant that one's future depended on the living of a good life which then determined the quality of their next incarnation. The life, in which one was stuck in at any given time, was called one's Karma. The fixed caste system that developed in India because of this goes back thousands of years, and, where a person would fit into that caste system was called their Ka.

Examples of The Way in Hindu Teachings

The demonic do things they should avoid and avoid the things they should do. Hypocritical, proud, and arrogant, living in delusion and clinging to their deluded ideas, insatiable in their desires, they pursue unclean ends.

Bound on all sides by scheming and anxiety, driven by anger and greed, they amass by any means they can a hoard of money for the satisfaction of their cravings. Self-important, obstinate, swept away by the pride of wealth, they ostentatiously perform sacrifices without any regard for their purpose. Egotistical, violent, arrogant, lustful, angry, envious of everyone, they abuse my presence within their own bodies and in the bodies of others. The Bhagavad Gita

Hell has three hates: lust, anger and greed.

He who has let go of hatred who treats all beings with kindness and compassion, who is always serene, unmoved by pain or pleasure... free of the "I" and "mine", self-controlled, firm and patient, his whole mind focused on me...that is the one I love best.

Now the one who does not desire – the one who is without desire and is freed from desire, whose desire is satisfied, whose desire is humility – his breaths do not depart. The Bhagavad Gita

People usually consider walking on water or in thin air a miracle. But I think the real miracle is not to walk either on water or in thin air, but to walk on earth. Every day we are engaged in a miracle which we don't even recognize: a blue sky, white clouds, green leaves, the black, curious eyes of a child -- our own two eyes. All is a miracle.

Through my love for you, I want to express my love for the whole cosmos, the whole of humanity, and all beings. By living with you, I want to learn to love everyone and all species. If I succeed in loving you, I will be able to love everyone and all species on Earth... This is the real message of love

We are here to awaken from our illusion of separateness.

Waking up this morning, I smile. Twenty-four brand new hours are before me. I vow to live fully in each moment and to look at all beings with eyes of compassion.

Because you are alive, everything is possible. Thich Nhat Hanh

Buddhism

As was true of Jesus of Nazareth, so it was true of Siddhartha Gautama, or as he later became called, *The Buddha* (563 to 486 BC). His intention, like Jesus, was not to start another religion. He just wanted to reform Hinduism from its superstitions and dehumanizing practices.

He was raised as a Hindu and enjoyed the benefits of being the son of a very wealthy Sakya clan Chief. His protected life was threatened when he discovered the poverty, disease and suffering of his people. Following his association with a holy man, Gautama set out to follow a path similar to this unusual man. At the age of 35, he became *a* buddha. To be called "*a* buddha" was the recognition of a person who had reached enlightenment. There were many men who were recognized as buddhas, but only Gautama was ever called *The* Buddha.

He rejected some of Hinduism such as: the caste system, the concept of many, many Gods, and the need to go through many rebirths (which demanded total submission to one's fate). He went out to teach what he called "The Middle Way." From his influence there evolved Four Sacred and Noble Truths, the last of which was to follow the Eight fold Path to Perfection (which involved the destruction of selfish desire).

He gathered many disciples and spent the next 45 years in Northeastern India spreading his word. Like Jesus, he insisted that he was no more than a humble servant of the people, and that he was not endowed with any unusual powers. However, after his death at Kushinagara when he was 85 years old, many myths began to spread. He too was made into a miracle worker, and like Jesus, he came to be looked upon as a God. Even though he wanted to reform Hinduism, he ended up being the founder of another of the world's great religions.

As was true of all religions, Buddhism spread to take on a multitude of forms. Surprisingly, it did not become the dominant religion of India because Gautama's radical reforms were never accepted in India. However it did become the dominant religion of China and remains so today.

The Hindu/Buddhist influence on the U.S and the West has been huge, but I'll mention two movements that I've studied and have meant something to me.

1. Transactional Analysis is a psycho-analytic theory, or method of therapy, developed by Eric Berne in the late 1950's. In it, social transactions are analyzed to determine the ego state of the patient (parent, adult, or child) that allow us to understand our behavior. Altering our ego state can then help us to deal with emotional problems. I'm OK – You're OK written by Thomas Anthony Harris in 1969 was the best selling and best received practical guide to

Transactional Analysis every written. It made the New York Times Best Seller list in 1972 and remained there for two years. It sold over 15 million copies. It is reported to be an offshoot of Buddhist teachings.

2. Maharishi Mahesh Yogi originated and founded Transcendental Meditation, that caused meditation as a whole to evolve into the U.S. and the West as a whole. In 1955 he publicly began teaching a technique that he learned from his teacher Brhamananda Saraswati, and he set up a teacher training program to enlist people to teach it to many more people, some of whom were celebrities. All of this encouraged scientific research that validated his technique and helped it to become popular it in the 1960's and 1970's. By the late twenty century, TM was being taught to millions and millions of people in a large multinational movement. There are still health and well-being programs being offered around the world, and there are still many schools and universities that teach its practice.

Examples of The Way in Buddhist Writings

(Because The Buddha and Jesus were so similar in their lives and teachings, I'm going to give you examples of some original teachings that they shared. If you would like to read more of these similarities, you can find them in a book edited by Marcus Borg called Jesus and Buddha, The Parallel Sayings.)

Consider others as yourself. Dhammapada 10

If anyone should give you a blow with his hand, with a stick, or with a knife, you should abandon any desire and utter no evil words. Majjhima Nikaya 21

Hatreds do not ever cease in this world by hating, but by love. This is an eternal truth...Overcome anger by love; overcome evil by good; overcome the miser by giving; overcome the liar by truth. Dhammapada 1 and 17

Abandoning the taking of life, the ascetic Gautama dwells refraining from taking life, without stick or sword. Digha Nikaya 1

If you do not tend one another, then who is there to tend you. Whoever would tend me, he should tend the sick. Vinaya, Mahavagga 8

The body of The Buddha is born of love, patience, gentleness and truth...The Bodhisattva loves all living beings as if each were his only child. Vamalakirtinirdesha Sutra 2 and 5

Just as a mother would protect her only child at the risk of her own life, cultivate a boundless heart towards all beings. Let your thoughts of boundless love pervade the whole world. Autta Nipata 149-150

Abstain from killing and from what is not given. Abstain from un-chastity and from speaking falsely. Do not accept gold and silver. Khuddakapatha 2

Taoism

Tao (pronounced "Dow") means path or way. As Confucius spoke of the way life *ought* to be, Lao Tzu (meaning the grand old teacher) gave equal weight to the way life *really is*. Lao Tzu (who many believe to be a legendary figure) wrote the Tao te Ching (meaning "The Way and its Power").

Taoism soon split into three branches: *Popular superstition* leaning on magic and sorcery; a complicated form of *mystical thinking*; and a *philosophy of the natural way* (nature's way) in which things work together to work themselves out.

It is the the teachings from the last form, that Taoism is now influencing the world . It has certainly influenced western culture. The expressions "go with the flow" and "if it ain't broke, don't fix it" come out of Taoism.

I must confess, as I said earlier, that the scripture of Taoism is one of my favorites. However in China, it evolved like all other religions, into pride and superstition. Still of the recent translations of all of the world's religious writings, the Tao te Ching written in 600 BC, may be the most popular. In the United States, it has increased in popularity through writers like Wayne Dyer, who was a famous psychologist, lecturer and author. He has written three best selling books on the <u>Tao te Ching</u> that are fascinating. The ideas of the Tao (the way) are simple yet complex, hard to understand yet obvious, and certainly profound and beautiful,. I believe that these words are touching and moving people to find The Way.

Examples of The Way in Taoism

(Remember that some examples can be found at the beginning of each chapter)

The Tao (The Way) that can be told is not the eternal Tao. The name that can be named is not the eternal name. The unnameable is the eternal real. Naming is the origin of all particular things. Free from desire, you realize the manifestations. Yet mystery and manifestations arise from the same source. This source is called darkness, the gateway to all understanding. Tao te Ching 1

The Tao (the Way) is like a well; used but never used up. It is like the eternal void; filled with infinite possibilities. It is hidden but always present. I don't know who gave birth to it. It's is older than The Source. Tao te Ching 4

Whoever is planted in the Tao (the Way) will not be rooted up. Whoever embraces the Tao will not slip away. Her name will be held in honor from generation to generation. Let the Tao be present in your life and you will become genuine. Let it be present in your family and your family will flourish. Let it be present in your country and your country will be an example to all countries in the world. Let it be present in the universe and the universe will sing. Tao te Ching 54

For governing a country well, there is nothing better than moderation. The mark of a moderate man is freedom from his own ideas. Tolerant like the sky, all- pervading like sunlight, firm like a mountain, supple like a tree in the wind, he has no destination in view and makes use of anything life happens to bring his way. Nothing is impossible for him because he has let go; he can care for the peoples welfare as a mother cares for her child. Tao te Ching 59

I have just three things to teach: simplicity, patience, compassion. These three are your greatest treasures. Simple in actions and in thoughts, you return to the source of being. Patient with both friends and enemies, you accord with the way things are. Compassionate toward yourself, you reconcile all beings in the world. Tao te Ching 67

Nothing in the world is as soft and yielding as water, yet for dissolving the hard and inflexible, nothing can surpass it. The soft overcomes the hard. The gentle overcomes the rigid. Everyone knows this is true, but few put it into practice. Therefore the master remains serene in the midst of sorrow. Evil cannot enter her heart, because she has given up helping; she is the people's greatest help.

This word seems paradoxical. Failure is an opportunity. If you blame someone else, there is no end to the blame. Therefore the master fulfills her own obligations and corrects her own mistakes. She does what she needs to do and demands nothing of others. Tao te Ching 78

I'm now going to conclude this study of religions, though there are numerous other religious writings I could use to demonstrate how *all* religions relate to The Way. For instance I could mention Sikhism, Confucianism, Shintoism, and others too numerous to list. However I do hope this has made the point.

(As I said earlier, If you want to study the subject of religions in greater depth, you can find it at the end of the book in Appendices III. Also you can read there about some of the religions I've left out.)

Poetry

Poetry, which is painting with words, reflects the fact that The Way can be found in all forms of beauty. If we look for The Way, it's clearly present in a lot of beautiful poetry. It's in so many poems that I don't know how I could ever just choose a few. What I really want to do is help you. through these few poems, to begin to see The Way in other poetry that you read. As I said, picking a few is silly...but here goes. Poems that immediately come to mind are:

Walk With Me
by Munda

Walk with me, the path of life,
 to explore every bend of the road
 Enjoy with me the beauty of life,
 along its wonderful way.

 Find comfort with me, in each other's arms
 when grief crosses our path.
 Find strength with me, in each other's
strength
 when despair lies in wait.

 Laugh with me a single true laugh
 to enlighten another's distress.
 Cry with me, a single true tear
 to understand true happiness.

 Cherish with me, the wonders of life,
 as they need to be preserved,
 Rejoice with me, in the mysteries
 of what is yet to be.

 Find peace with me, in each other's souls,
 when the world has gone insane
 Find love with me, in each other's hearts,
 until this life has been fulfilled.

 And when the path comes to an end
 I hope we can say from within
 We've known the beauty of true love,
 our love came from within

Flowers, dear Flowers Farewell
Louisa May Alcott

We are sending you, dear flowers,
Forth alone to die,
Where your gentle sisters may not weep
O'er the cold graves where you lie;
But you go to bring them fadeless life
In the bright homes where they dwell,
And you softly smile that 'tis so,
As we sadly sing farewell.

O plead with gentle words for us,
And whisper tenderly
Of generous love to that cold heart,
And it will answer ye;
And though you fade in a dreary home,
Yet loving hearts will tell
Of the joy and peace that you have given:
Flowers, dear flowers, farewell.

The Road Not Taken
By Robert Frost

Two roads diverged in a yellow wood,
And sorry I could not travel both
And be one traveler, long I stood
And looked down one as far as I could
To where it bent in the undergrowth;

Then took the other, as just as fair
And having perhaps the better claim,
Because it was grassy and wanted wear;
Though as for that the passing there
Had worn them really about the same,
And both that morning equally lay

In leaves no step had trodden black.
Oh, I kept the first for another day!
Yet knowing how way leads on to way,
I doubted if I should ever come back.

I shall be telling this with a sigh
Somewhere ages and ages hence:
Two roads diverged in a wood, and I —
I took the one less traveled by,
And that has made all the difference.

Evening
Emily Dickinson

She sweeps with many-colored brooms,
And leaves the shred behind,
Oh housewife in the evening west,
Come back, and dust the pond!
You dropped a purple raveling in,
You dropped an amber thread;
And now you've littered all the East
With duds of emerald!
And still she plies her spotted brooms,
And still the aprons fly,
Till brooms fade softly into stars-
And then I come away.

W. H. Auden

Defenseless under the night
Our world in stupor lies;
Yet dotted everywhere,
Ironic points of light
Flash out wherever the just
Exchange their messages;
May I, composed like them

Of Eros and of dust,
Beleaguered by the same
Negation and despair,
Show an affirming flame.

(I'd like to close with a poem I wrote in a book of poetry.)

Wander Not Alone
Michal Hall

Wander not alone,
The real path is darkened by our night,
and we are lost,
And true, false guides seduce us from the paths
we know are real,
And we know the signs we follow now
will be gone tomorrow.
So wander not alone.

To wander lost together far exceeds the lone abyss,
To touch another's hand does temper
so the darkness,
And to hear a muffled sound does
herald in such hope.
Call out…stand and listen,
Someone may be close enough to hear
and turn your way,
Someone, even now, may be searching
out your trail,
Reach out to find that gentle voice
whispering in the darkness,
Touch it, embrace it, love it,
And forever, wander not alone.

The appreciation of poems is a very personal thing, so don't be offended if what I've chosen here does not please you. The point is that we can see flashes of beauty and truth in so many poems that can point us to The Way. Personally I love poetry and enjoy writing it. I've also been amazed by its power to help us sense humility, love, and lasting beauty

Prose

There are quite a few nonfiction books and articles that continue to point us to The Way, but I'm sorry to say that lately I've found this in fewer and fewer books of fiction. I think that's because nonfiction often reaches for some ideal that's mystical and unknown, while fiction is usually searching for, or trying to depict, what is real right now (and that now tends to be most unpleasant). However I would never say that all fiction is devoid of inspiring stories that point us toward The Way, because I've read some recently that would disprove that statement. It is possible that the moral and ethical drop in modern fiction is coming out of evolving pride with its greed, power, violence and war that have nothing to do with The Way. However because The Way is still in everything, there will always be works of fiction that rise above our sordid mess to allow compassion and peace to peek out.

1.

I'm not going to list a large number of **nonfiction** authors because there are far too many of them that direct us toward The Way, however I'll list a few that for me were significant. I've already mentioned people who have touched my life like Teilhard de Chardin, Thomas Merton, Wayne Dyer, Dwayne Elgin, John Philip Newell, Thich Nhat Hanh, Deepak Chopra and Eckhart Tolle. I could go on, but I won't because the ones who've touched me may not touch you. I'll leave you to search from the abundant possibilities available to you to find nonfiction that is of value to you in your journey toward The Way.

2.

I'll also not list a lot of books of *fiction* or give you a vast lists of authors, because I really don't really know that many. However I do hope that you can look for your own favorites that include influences of The Way. However having said that, I can't resist offering a few authors that come to mind like: Charles Dickens, Victor Hugo, Carson McCullough, F. Scott Fitzgerald, Harper Lee, Elizabeth Gilbert, Cathryn Stockett, Sara Gruen, Eowyn Ivey, or Abraham Verghese. Once again I'll leave it up to you and move on.

3.

You could also say that *stage and television* stories (which come from written scripts) can also reflect The Way. Of course books, stage and television are dependent on the audience's reaction, and most of the time that reaction is mired in the pride and greed that brings forth things like gross sexuality, violence with explosions, anger, hate and revenge. All of that certainly doesn't gel with The Way, and I believe it pushes our evolution backwards. Audience's violent, irrational reactions, that add to our overpopulation and pollution of the Earth, are then fed back to further erode the ethics of television, movies, and the stage. Now, especially in movies and video games, violence rules. It's all vicious circle where violence is presented because of audience demand, to then teach the audience to be more violence, to then demand more of it. Thus it is increasingly hard for The Way to be found anywhere in the modern world. However we should never loose sight of the fact that The Way is not gone. Its still right there where it's always been, at the heart of the cosmos and within our tarnished hearts.

The point of all of this is that the written word can at times help us to see The Way. I've already demonstrated how religious scriptures and their other writings are full of The Way. Still I must say that no writing can presently be free of pride's pollution because that's who we are. Still clear evidence of The Way will always remain within us and around us, if we can be open enough to see it.

Science

I always say that my studies of science may have helped me to see The Way. Science is essentially free of superstition because of its empirical approach that is not as infected by pride. Pride can raise its ugly head in science, but just not as often. Cosmology teaches us to be humble, which is essential to perceiving The Way, and if we can become humble (free of pride),The Way opens to us. It could be argued that all of the various disciplines of Science could help us to see The Way, so I'll speak about a few that have also helped me.

Let me say that I have no patience with those who still find science to be evil or bad, because clearly it is a recently evolved discipline that helps us to understand ourselves and the cosmos from which we've come. As beings who are made to reflect on ourselves and everything around us, I think we *de*-volve when we shy away from using science's educational disciplines. Science should be a cherished friend and constant companion, and it has become just that to me. I believe that superstitions, coming from religions and elsewhere, can keep us from concentrating on the truths that science has revealed. For instance some superstitions may teach us that a God can solve all of our problems so we should ignore them because God will deal with them. For instance the fact that we are going extinct is ignored despite all of the massive evidence. I also see superstitions blocking our reflection, education, evolution and even our future. Superstitions can make us discount and ignore the great gift of wisdom that is science today. They can even allow us to deny who we are as a reflective analytical species, rape the Earth with our pride and greed, destroy the plants, animals and ecosystems, and ultimately cease to be.

I am far from an expert, and I would never call myself a "scientist". I would see myself as more of an admirer who is always open and eager to learn more. Thus I'm asking you to bear with me as I pass on some things I've learned about science, so that maybe you can take up this amazing study for yourself.

There are hundreds of different kinds of science. However they are sometimes put into categories such as:

Natural sciences: the study of natural phenomena (including the fundamental and biological life)

Formal sciences: the study of mathematics and logic that uses an a priori, as opposed to factual, methodology

Social sciences: the study of human behavior and societies.

Applied sciences: applying existing scientific knowledge to develop more practical applications (like healthcare, technology or inventions).

It would be impossible to talk about all of the multitude of scientific branches that come from these labels, so I'll only choose the ones I've found to be the most helpful in my evolution toward The Way. I recognize that these may not be as helpful to you as some other aspect of science, and even science itself may not be the best avenue in your journey, because we all come to The Way along different paths.

Cosmology

Cosmology, the study of the vast cosmos, is perhaps my favorite science because, more than anything else, it has taught me to be humble and amazed before something that is so much bigger, complex and unknowable than myself, and this has moved me closer to The Way. Cosmology says that we began with the amazing explosion of what science calls a "singularity". This explosion called "The Big Bang" occurred 13.7 billion years ago. After it, quarks evolved into photons, positron and neutrinos, and hadrons formed neutrons, protons, and electrons to ultimately become atoms. This, with the help of bosons, allowed what we call "matter" to evolve into being For the next 300 thousand years everything cooled and expanded to come together to form Helium, hydrogen and lithium. After this, matter, light and radiation separated from the mix to go their separate ways. We could go on and on with this, but, if you're interested, look it up.

By the way, matter is energy moving slowly, and energy is matter moving quickly ($E=MC2$), so what we, and all matter, are is energy. We are made up of atoms which are made up of things like electrons, protons, and neutrons. We've evolved from the Big Bang as well as the star's dust from explosions, and more recently we've evolved from the planet Earth. Thus we are energy from the Big Bang, dust from the stars; and the evolution of the Earth.

We now also know that our planet is far from the only one out there (which was the belief up until several hundred years ago), and just recently we've learned that we are far from the only planet in the cosmos capable of evolving life. From very recent discoveries, we've also found that there are an impossible-number-to-count planets out there in the cosmos. This means that without question there are a lot of these planets (like our Earth) that are close enough to a star to have water that does not to freeze, and far enough away not to boil, which would allow the evolution of life. Also the size of the cosmos is so great (impossible to imagine) with its unknowable trillions upon trillions of planet out there there so there is no question that *even reflective life* is evolving all over the cosmos.

However the shocking distance between stars means that there is no way, with our present technology, to get close enough to another solar system to even communicate with radio waves. Also it is probably impossible for one of these other planets to ever be able to communicate with us for the same reason. The cosmos is just too big for anything we now know about to travel quickly enough through space-time to communicate with another planet.

I could go on with this because I find this aspect of who we are to be fascinating, however I'll stop here because I want to ask you a question I asked earlier. "How does all of this make you feel? Does it make you feel small; does it make you feel scared; does it make you want to shout at me to stop?" I've have had people respond in all of these ways...but why? I think it's because they feel threatened. I also think the answer comes from our being enmeshed in the renegade emotion of pride which makes us want to hold onto the belief that *we* are the center of everything everywhere. If we do accept the amazing wonders of the cosmos, it becomes obvious that we aren't the center of anything! That's why studying cosmology might mean that we are pushed out of our pride enough to see a glimpse of humility and thus have a chance of perceiving The Way.

The new studies on Dark Matter and Dark Energy (named "dark" because we can't see them) are shocking because Dark Matter makes up 68% of the cosmos and Dark Energy makes up 27%, so what we see and know is only 5% of the cosmos. Also the expansion and sheer size of the cosmos underlines the fact that the cosmos is total mystery. However it does appear that our discovery of Dark Matter would affirm the accepted theory that the cosmos will ultimately come together to form another singularity that can explode again. However we now know that the cosmos is *not* coming together... and we know why. It's now thought to be expanding because of the discovery of Dark Energy. We can now see that this means that the cosmos is being fueled to drift apart until it is torn apart or freezes. Look at this...it means that the cosmos is totally beyond us. It's far beyond our wildest imaginings and far outside of our mental reach. Also recent studies have revealed further that what we can see with all of our various telescopes through the billions of stars that make up our galaxy is only a tiny slice of the cosmos. Thus we'll never be able to see what's out there and the cosmos will remain a mystery. Because of all of this, I've think that to study or even think-about the cosmos should make us dizzy as we experience the humble-shock of its magnitude. Also I have believe that whenever we move toward a humble state of mind, we are automatically moving toward The Way because that's what happened to me. Studying the cosmos to wipe out my ingrained pride?control myths really did help me to see The Way and write this book.

Sub-atomic Theory

Let's move on and talk about the evolving ideas coming out of Subatomic Theory. Most people tend to link it with the study of the cosmos, however cosmology looks up at what's huge, while subatomic theory looks down at what's microscopic. However they both teach us about things that are real and about who we really are.

I confess that on the subject of subatomic theory, I'm even less of an expert. It's really over my head, but I'll struggle to pass on to you a few threads of what I understand. Most people have heard of and affirm that everything is made up of atoms that are made up of rotating energy such as protons, electrons and neutrons. Thus as I said earlier, everything is energy (because matter is energy moving slowly, while energy is matter moving quickly). As this basic energy at the core of who we are has been studied, we have found that it does some really strange things. For instance, it appears and disappears in different places, and it can even be in two places at once.

Quantum (subatomic) theories about the strong nuclear force are called Chromodynamics. It describes the interactions of sub-nuclear particles such as gluons and quarks. The weak nuclear force and the electromagnetic force are unified into a single quantum field theory know as the electoweak theory. However, it has proved difficult to construct quantum models beside what we call gravity (the remaining fundamental force in the cosmos) because of huge differences in matter's general relativity and the fundamental assumptions of subatomic theory. However this problem has recently been addressed in a new theory. Einstein spent the last years of his life trying to find a "theory of everything" that would incorporate both gravitational and subatomic forces, but he never succeeded. However it now appears that we may be approaching it.

This theory is called "*string theory*" and is very new. It first said that everything is made up of vibrating strings of energy that vibrate in different ways to create all that exists. It presented a romantic picture of everything vibrating like a giant orchestra with different instruments presenting a harmonious whole. It was quite fetching and well received, but before long it came into question because five other string theories were presented alongside the first that had equal credibility.

The "M Theory" is now trying to bring all of the string theories together. Also through our senses, we can only pick up 4 dimensions of reality (that we call height, depth, width and time), but this new theory says that there are actually *ten* dimensions. Also recently, mathematicians and physicists have postulated another dimension, to bring the total to *eleven*. M theory sees all of the string theories to be something like small islands floating upon the ocean of a yet fully to be hashed-out reality. Parts of this theory say that there may be many other vibrating membrane-universes (called "multi-verses") out there, and some of them may be very much like ours and even contain universes that are parallel to our own.

I need to say that both cosmic theory and subatomic theory are "theories". This means that we're looking at things that we can't see or fully even comprehend. The cosmos is way too big for us to see all of it, while subatomic particles are way too small for us to see at all. Thus we must rely on theories that are backed-up by other disciplines such as mathematics and physics to give us ideas about them.

As I've also said, both of these studies make us stretch our minds to face the scary reality of our incredible smallness and lack of importance, and this flies in the face of what we've all been taught from birth. Of course it also introduces us to some real humility that is fundamental to, and leads us to, The Way. Perhaps with this humility, we can start traveling down the road to see and maybe even be The Way. Of course this can only happen when we are no longer escaping reality with prideful superstitious and cover-ups, to be able to turn around and face the humble truth of our interconnected state of being. Also then we will be able to see what I call "the cosmic ethic" that can be perceived by recently evolved reflective beings in the cosmos, which they must see and choose if they are to survive.

Social Sciences

I feel that psychology, sociology and anthropology are all related. They share many things in common since they are concerned about present or past human interactions. I am linking them together because when I studied them in college and have continued to study them, I've come to see how they interact with, and are concerned about, the same things from a different perspective.

Psychology

Psychology is defined as the science of the mind and human interaction that defines the mental and behavioral characteristics of an individual. I found that our mental and behavioral activities, that are generally put into shallow categories like good or bad, nice or mean, or cruel or humane, are a lot more than that. Now they are mostly relegated to simple, non-reflective slogans or stereotypes, when the truth is that mental and behavioral activities are extremely complex just because of our complex brains, our different environments, our various religious and educational experience, and a lot of other things. It's only with the evolution of psychology that we've stepped out to try to understand our actions. We've now studied human behaviors, and started making some sense of them; we've studied the brain and how it works; and we've studied our emotions with their vitality, danger and tenderness. Yet even with all of the many revelations that have followed, we still remain in the dark about much of our behavior as a species. Also large numbers of people know nothing of these studies and even believe them to be crazy. They associate psychology with superstition, quackery and intellectual gumbo-jumbo and then quickly discard it.

Since my first college courses in psychology, I've found it to be fascinating. With its controlled, logical scientific methods, I've seen how you really can make sense out of complicated behavioral patterns to better understand (and have sympathy for) ourselves and others around us. It's helped me to be far less condemnatory and judging, and to be a more logical person about everything. I've become more aware and interested in people and their problems to better be able to talk with them and understand the complex wonder of humanity's interactions. Psychology's wisdom has drawn me closer to other people to allow me to enter into their lives, which has also greatly helped me to understand and see The Way.

Sociology

I also took some courses in both sociology and anthropology. Sociology is the study of society, social institutions, and social relationships. When I systematically learned from this science, I was able to see the development, structure and function of human groups, and see the organized patters of our collective behavior. This allowed me to be more appreciative of other cultures different from my own, and more comfortable participating in all human groupings. I was also amazed at how sociology can even help us to predict how societies (groups and individuals) might interact with one another. All of this come from and is based upon carefully collected data.

Anthropology

Anthropology looks at humanity by examining its past from from the historical and archaeological records. It studies humans in relation to distribution, origin, classification, racial relationships, physical characteristics, environment, social interactions, and culture. It is sometimes even said to teach us about the origin, nature and destiny of humanity, as it reveals things that have happened in the past to clarify what might happen in the future . Of course it's best known for its archaeological digs where earth is carefully sifted to find, analyze and classify past relics.

All of these sciences can help us to remove superstitions based on our mindless pride, and can help us focus on findings that teach us humility to helps us move toward The Way. Pride itself is a myth, so humility is who we really are and meant to be. I believe that unpolluted science naturally lead us to humility to be where we belong... in The Way. These sciences can really be helpful as their careful logic lights our way to truth.

I could go on to look at many more scientific disciplines such as: biology, botany, chemistry, entomology, geology, microbiology, physics, paleontology, pathology, zoology, and others. All of these sciences are fascinating, and have swarms of books written about them. They too can help us to be humble and approach The Way. Of course being informed and even adept at science is not the only potential avenue for us to come out of pride and see The Way, but for me it's been a very helpful and powerful one.

Hope and fear are both phantoms
that arise from thinking of the self.
When we don't see the self as self,
what do we have to fear?
See the world as your self.
Have faith in the way things are.
Love the world as your self;
then you can care for all things. Tao te Ching

VI. What *Pursuing*
The Way Could Mean

Part I . A Review

You have to admit that right now our life as human beings ranges from difficult horrible. Who cannot look around and see how miserable we are in our greed, violence, militancy and competition. For a reflective species, we have not reflected enough to coexist with each other, our brother and sister species in life's ecosystems or the Earth. Scientists and others who've studied this are saying that because of our run-away overpopulation and disregard for each other and the Earth, we will soon be extinct. Come on!...don't you think something is wrong? Also wouldn't you agree that we need to find a way to right this battered ship right now.

Some think that religion with its various gods, myths and saints can help, so they've offered them their full support through their participation, money, and enthusiasm. Others reach out to popular psychiatrists who write best selling books about things we can do to find happiness and success, while others seek hope in politics and various organizations (such as military or civic groups). This search is always on, but nothing has been found that really offers a solution.

Psychologically, for a little while, things may seem to help. However when we look around and see who we've become and the awful mess we've made, we have to return to reality and admit that nothing has changed nothing and they just aren't enough. We're still stuck in our old prideful, destructive, unhappy lives in the same lethal environment.

"Ah", you say, " now here's *another* meaningless suggestion on what we can do." Well, I can see how you might feel that way, but you're wrong. I would never want to be labeled as someone trying push another religion, movement, group, or easy solution, because that's not what The Way is about. The Way is just there. It's right in front of us all the time, but we've ignored it and missed it. The answer to our problems has always always been there in front of us, around us, within us and a part of us, because the answer to our problems is to first enter the power of The Way. In fact The Way has been and is a part of everything since it's lodged within the evolution of the cosmos as it brings everything together. Thus in our reflective evolution, we should have long ago been able to reflect on it, and be a part of it. We should certainly by now have seen it in the obvious code of ethics that underlies us. We should understand that the main difference in our evolution as a reflective species from other species is that we are able to choose, but what we have chosen is not The Way. Also The Way is not something that we have to invent, find or even discover, because it's already there. All we have to do is stop ignoring it.

I also believe that The Way is an amazing, mystical ethic that has inspired religious writers, poets, and sages over the years, and that it really can be the savior of our species. With the guidance of The Way, *we* can save ourselves, and that's because *we* are now the ones destroying ourselves. I firmly believe that if we continue to ignore The Way and continue on our present path, we will continue our drift into darkness to know even more misery and destruction.

Part 2. Beginning to Move

Even if we just approach The Way, it still starts to offer us the tools to build an anchored, stable, and meaningful existence. Of course if anyone can move towards its glow, they'll find themselves moving toward a life of peace, security, hope, and stability. They will begin to see how everyone can be fulfilled as they contribute to each other, the Earth and the cosmos. They'll see how the Earth will reconstitute and heal itself as we stop our prideful overpopulation, pollution and destruction of the animals and plants, which will offer our species, and all species on the Earth, a meaningful, joyous, long future. In other words as we approach The Way, we begin to be real to be set free to use our reflective gifts appropriately as they were meant to be used

In attempting to use a few more limited human words to describe this, I could say we will begin to enter the amazing state of humility and love that embraces the peace and justice of everyone and everything. We will begin to live without worry or guilt, without comparing or competition, without fear or anger, without revenge or violence. We will begin to experience never trying to control anyone or anything, but thorough compromise and cooperation, start empowering everything around us. Our nature would begin to be sharing rather than hoarding, cherishing life rather than wasting it, and of course to loving...really loving. As we love, we will begin to welcome everything in, rather than fearing it to shut everything out. We will start welcoming life rather than fighting it to soar naturally into the vast, ageless evolution of the cosmos. We'll begin to see that our present state of disaster is coming from being minimized and ripped apart by arrogance, greed, control and the abuse of power that make it impossible for us to imagine who we could and should be with relationships of humility and love that naturally come from The Way.

Of course there are some instances where people or groups have tried to imagine such things. For instance, Judaism speaks of "The Day of the Lord" or "the coming of the Messiah"; Christians speak of "The Kingdom of God"; Buddhist talk about "Nirvana"; Taoism talks about "The Tao" (The Way) and Shintoism talks about "The Way of the Source". We dream about things like "Shanghai-La", "Bali-Hi", "Brigadoon" or "Xanadu". Various social experiments, such as communes or The Social Gospel, could also be said to be examples. All of these are reaching for a more healthy place to be in the darkness we now share together. Of course I believe that what we're really searching for is The Way.

Part 3. Imagining The Way

If I were to naively make a stab at what following The Way might look like, it would be where we all see *everything* (every person, species, and the cosmos itself) as being just as important, just as deserving of respect, and just as miraculous as ourselves...as being one. It would be where we would love everyone and everything as much as we love ourselves, so we could never harm another life form or any of the natural evolutions of the Earth. It would be where there are *no* boundaries or borders, groupings or stereotypes, judgments or acts of greed. Everyone would be seen as equal to cooperate and encourage, rather than compete and out-do. The Earth would be accepted as our real home, and we would have a cosmic consciousness where we stood in awe of, and were thankful for, all of the known and unknown things that make up our lives, the Earth and the cosmos. We would see all of the Earth's life forms as family, and we would love the Earth as our mother.

In our work, we would not be motivated by money and greed, but by a natural desire to contribute and encourage all of evolution (rather than tragically fighting against it). There would be no competition because everyone would be trying to maximize the talents of the other for the good of all. With humility (rather than pride) underlying who we are, we would never know loneliness, fear, guilt, worry, revenge, or any other pride-induced emotions. Our time would be spent trusting, loving, supporting, encouraging, and helping, rather than being suspicious, fearing, fighting, and struggling with everything.

I could go on and on with this but I do think such imaginings may help us to perceive The Way. We have evolved far away from what a reflective, intelligent evolution should be, but we can't give up. The answer is still within us and around us. Right now we can step out of our pride and step into The Way to regain our authentic selves and live a viable future. The question is will we?

He who stands on tiptoe
doesn't stand firm.
He who rushes ahead
doesn't go far.
He who tries to shine
dims his own light
He who defines himself
can't know who he really is.
He who has power over others
can't empower himself.
He who clings to his work
will create nothing that endures.
If you want to accord with The Way,
just do your job, and then let go. Tao te Ching

VII. Being The Way

Part 1. Becoming The Way

When we can perceive The Way and enter it, we *become* The Way. It's not really something that can be taught, talked about, or even done. It's just something that we become...who we are. The Way is not a thing or a place, and it's not something to grow into. It's not a thing at all, because it's more like a life-style of being connected to and a part everything in the cosmos. Of course this is who we really are, and have been all along, and it's who we must be to survive. However The Way is much more than all of that. It has to do with being able to "be" rather than just "exist", as we're now doing in this deviate evolution carved out of pride, arrogance, separation and violence.

For most of my life I was a member and leader of a religious community. I said that I "believed" in God. However you can't say that you "believe" in The Way. To believe in some-*thing* means that that you think it is some thing, but The Way is not a thing. To make it into a thing is to tie it down to us or some-thing like matter or energy. However we can't do that because The Way is not in any way like us or anything that we can tie down and name. No, it's really an underlying aspect of the cosmos that is directing everything together into the future. It's a presence that is in everything, as well a presence in us that we must enter to survive. We can't believe in it, but what we can do is *be* it. When we understand that, enlightenment will begin to takes us out of ourselves (our confining sense of self) to *be* The Way.

The way does not care what you call it, or whether you stand in awe and worship it. It doesn't care if we use human words like "follow", "accept", "become" or anything else to describe how we enter it or receive it. The Way does not get its feelings hurt and get get angry, jealous, revengeful or anything else that we prideful humans do (which are also ascribed to our humanized god-myths). The Way is just there, and we as reflective beings must accept it to *bring us all together*, as it does with everything else in the cosmos. As I've said, human words are not important when we approach The Way, because it's far, far beyond anything human.

Part 2. Being and Non-being

I have always been fascinated by that ontological statement of Shakespeare, "To be or not to be; that is the question." I've found that "being" is not just being alive; it's also being on track with the cosmos and its moral ethic. As I've said, I believe that The Way is the map, direction and grounding of all reflective beings that we must choose if we are to evolve safely and well. I also believe that humility and love (which come from The Way that moves us together) are manifestations of our "being", while pride and hate separate us and are manifestations of our "non-being". Thus if we want to "be", we have to enter the kingdom of The Way's "yes" that brings life, but if we want to "not be", we can continue to live in pride's dark, life-draining kingdom of the "no" that knows only death.

Therefore when I say we will *be* The Way, I'm saying more than just our being a part of something – no, we're literally *being* The Way. I'm referring to a time when we've entered The Way to *be...*

to be who we really are and live. This means that everything we say and everything we do is natural, easy and real. We don't have to think about it, analyze it, or even be aware of it, because it's who we are (and who we've really always been), We become a being of The Way to at last be home. It also means that we make our decisions, and base our lives, on what I call the "ground of being" (which is The Way). Thus we no more make decisions on the basis of pride's brainwashed nonsense. For instance we don't just vote for a political party; we vote using our own reflective abilities to decide who will be closest to The Way. We don't just think and do what our national leaders or nations tell us; we decided for ourselves how we will act and live closest to The Way. We don't allow popularity, social class, stereotypes, traditions, or anything else to take priority over our being The Way, because The Way has become who we are.

Part 3. Who We Are

I believe that we as reflective beings are now having a nervous breakdown. We are lost. This is because 10 to 15 thousand years ago in our evolution on this planet, we evolved to a place where we could see and consciously move into The Way. However (as we do now) we discarded The Way's uniting humility, love and peace. to chose instead divisive pride's greed, hate and arrogance. Ever since, we have been going more and more insane! We can first see it in the way that tribes, or groups of tribes, began fighting with each other over prideful things like rights to land, revenge, jealousy, or the desire for power, In the same way, we've used our new found technical knowledge to wage massive insane wars that are unimaginatively disastrous to both sides, murderous and an insult to all things decent. This blind ignorance is further seen in the way that war is now affirmed, celebrated and even encouraged. However this same insanity is also now seen in the technological advances that are energized by dirty, cheep energy to pollute the air, water, and land, and in the way that we're wiping out the animals and plants to destroy the ecosystems of the Earth. All of this inspired by prideful greed is driving us into extinction. Pride and greed are also behind our inability to even address our sick overpopulation as we worship of our wealth and our "progress".

Many believe that our extinction as a species is irreversible... and justly so. However I believe that The Way that is still in us, and that offers us some hope,..because all we have to do is recognize it and become it Still even if we don't do this and go extinct, some of the other reflective beings out there in the cosmos *will* evolve naturally in The Way and survive into the future. They will never have chosen divisive pride to move them out of The Way. No, they will have rejected "non-being" to choose the yes of being that is unaffected by the dying kingdom of pride's "no". They are even now rejoicing in the living realm of The Way's "yes" and will continue to be secure, happy and well. *(If all of this ontological talk sounds too philosophical and weird, I'm sorry. It's because I'm a great admirer of Paul Tillich's book* The Courage To Be*, and Douglas John Hall's book* The Stewardship of Life in the Kingdom of Death.*)*

We shouldn't give up because we are still a part of the evolving cosmos, and the cosmos has a long, long way to go. In addition, each one of us still is a functioning part of the miraculous wonder of reflection, (I would also add that we can't know the times or seasons because we have zero ability to predict the future.) Thus as a reflective, aware, and supposedly intelligent species with The Way embedded, we can't possibly know how we might respond or change in the next one or two hundred years. With our amazing brains that are brim full of consciousness, we are certainly capable of reversing at any time this idiotic course we've chosen. I've said over and over that everything in the cosmos is evolving, so maybe you and I can start evolving (instead of devolving) to be a productive, contributing, sustainable species in the cosmos. Who knows?

All we can now do is continue to seek and find The Way with great gusto. In spite of all the blocks, we must try to break through and become The Way. We must enter this powerful ethic and be a real, decent and sustainable cosmic beings...and we must never, ever give up! We needn't care what other people say, what groups we offend, or how far we veer off some predetermined, prideful norm. No, what we need to do is just be who we really are and who we're meant to be (which is The Way), and then live out whatever is left of our humble, loving, free existence.

I believe from my own experience that just searching for and moving toward The Way lifts us out of the trivialities of pride's divisions and delusions to experience life for the first time. As a part of nature and the Earth, we are made to smoothly evolve. We're not only made to know the wonder of life, but also the miracle of reflective life. We're made to enjoy each day that our lives have to offer, as we bask in the glory of our four amazing senses brought together by our complex brains to allow us to comprehend what's within and without. We are made to rejoice in the wonder of the massive, ever evolving cosmos, and appreciate and contribute to the vast everything in which we exist. Yes, we are especially made to rejoice in this ever evolving Earth that has been so graciously placed before us.

In other words, we should not just be painfully looking at our deviant evolution. We should also not just be wasting our lives cowering in fear as we try to tranquilize everything away. No, we should be living, loving and enjoying it. I believe that our clear, uncomplicated, commonsense wisdom, that is still within us, can allow us to reach The Way and live. If we do, The Way will open to us windows of truth that lift us far beyond ourselves where we can see things differently and enter into all that lies outside the walls of pride's slavery. This experience of "being" will leave us relaxed, free of divisions, and centered on what's important. Things like guilt, worry, comparing, competition, fear, anger, and fighting (with ourselves and others) will fade away as we evolve for the rest of our lives into the eternal wisdom of The Way.

Part 4. Choosing Reality

Since you've read this book, for the first time you should now have a choice. You can make a critical decision you couldn't make before because you were locked in pride. Now you can either choose to become The Way and taste the wonder of this unifying, cosmic ethic, or you can continue to wallow in the selfishness of pride and greed to taste the misery of separation, loneliness, and violence. It's your choice.

Of course to make this choice is not easy. I know because I've personally found it to be extremely difficult. I think it's because that, even though I was brought up by parents who clearly appreciated The Way's influence through their religion, I found it hard to give up the familiar kingdom of death (pride) that's always been a part of me and who I've evolved to be.

I found it especially hard to give up the community that I found in my religion. However now I'm finding a wider and more amazing community in presences that have always been around me but, since I was locked within myself, I couldn't see. I'm now finding this community all around me as I grow in my awareness of other people, the life of plants and animals, and the mystical Earth, solar system, galaxy, and cosmos that have created me and sustained me. In addition, since I'm now older and can't travel the Earth as much to witness its cherished communities, I have more time to visit them and my fellow creatures across the world through my books and the stimulation of the senses we call television. Thus I now have community, but just in a different way.

I also rejoice that having seen The Way and beginning to live within it, I now feel liberated to rejoice in the humility, love, kindness and peace I've found that allows me feel real. For the first time I can feel myself becoming who I really am.

Part 5. A Personal Word

Before we end this discussion, grant me a personal word. When I teach about all of this, some people ask me why my writings are so negative. I reply first by saying that I don't think The Way is in any way negative, in fact I believe that it's the most positive subject I've approached. I admit that the fact that we're going extinct is negative, but then, that's just a fact. It's a documented fact that points to who we are and have become.

Some people insist that *over*population (coming from too many births and the huge advances in healthcare) is not a fact because overpopulation is not really a problem (as is also said about global warming) because we have so much unused space on the Earth, and births have begun to slow. I point out that the dangers of overpopulation have nothing to do with how much unused space is left on the Earth (most of which is uninhabitable), but it has to do with our increasing destruction of the ecosystems that are now dying. I also point out that though there has recently been a slight drop in our population's advanced, scientists agree that we will still grow from 7 billion to 9 billion in 20 years, so obviously overpopulation, which is now preposterous, will just get worse...and yes, that's negative and not good.

Also others have said that we're not going extinct because we have plenty of time to use our amazing technology to fix our problems. I encourage them to look at the fact that presently our technology is only making things worse, and we have no evidence that this situation, that is inspired by greed, will change. Many scientists, after much evaluation, say that we will be extinct in 200 to 1200 years, and one of our most outstanding scientist says that he can prove that it will be in just 100 years. In other words we don't have enough *time* to wait (as we're now doing) thinking that maybe one day somebody will fix. We need wake up and realize that we're running out of time! I've found that if we can look at this rationally, free ourselves from escapism, and admit that both our present and future are frightening, it is actually a great relief. That's because we don't have to pretend anymore, and we can join with others who are really trying to do something about this.

I've also had people ask me why I want to write at all. I've replied that I enjoy writing, and I like to search what is true...and that's not easy today because there's so little truth around. I find that when I write, it's a little like being a detective in a television program like Murder She Wrote, Agatha Christie or Father Brown, where they are always finding themselves in the middle of a crime scene trying to solve it. I constantly find myself in crime scenes trying to solve them. However with this book is different, because I've been able to see something wonderful and inspiring, while also witnessing a much deeper, more ignored, and evil villain in the crimes I address. I can now see that discarding The Way to enter sick pride is what underlies *all* of our many horrible crimes. We should by now be aware that *we are the ones responsible* for the crimes of the murder of each other, other life forms on the Earth, and out future. We should also know what the *motive of our crimes* are, because we can see how we have pushed aside the cosmic ethic of The Way, to replace it with the sick ethic of arrogance and greed.

I believe that the reason The Way's teachings on love and humility that are scattered throughout the world's religions have been ignored has to do with motivation. Religions have tried to motivate with superstitions...with things like pleasing some human-like myth to go to heaven and meet loved ones, or, in the East, coming back from death in a better state. It does appear that the majority of religious people have never really believed these motivations, and their actions have reflected that fact. However the motivation for entering The Way is sensible and straight forward. It is free of pride's superstition, judgment, or guilt, to be replace by something that brings us together to live with each other, and other species, in humble, loving, kind, and peaceful relationships. Of course recently we've been made aware of another motivation. We are motivated to enter The Way as we admit that our overpopulation and pollution is killing off the Earths ecosystems to destroy not only the plants and animals, but all of us as well. .We are motivated when we see that we have to do something immediately to save our species, and also to live in loving, secure, sharing relationships with each other and the Earth, so our descendants will able to live. (Yes, survival is no small motivation!)

Still the good news (not negative news) is that The Way continues to be right here. Thus there is no logical reason why as reflective beings we should not see it, choose it, enter it, and become it. There is no reason that having become The Way, we cannot evolve to quickly use our reflective gifts (reflecting out and reflecting in) to wipe away this tragic detour. This detour began ten thousand years ago as we embraced the foolishness of arrogance, pride and greed to evolve into this insane pride culture. There is no reason we can't move out of this chaos to regain the evolution of The Way into wisdom, humility, love and peace. There is no reason why we can't use the glorious gifts of education, travel, and everyone's and everything's (including the Earth's) wisdom to know real inner and outer peace to continue our evolution into the cosmos as a responsible, positive beings.

Of course we will have to stop talking and start doing. Things people do now about the environment (like recycling, reducing emissions, and trying to limit fishing, deforestation, animal slaughter abuse, and energy waste) are all good things, but they cannot in themselves make a real difference. Remember almost all of air pollution (and most water pollution) comes from factories and power-plants that are seen as necessary for our prideful standard of living that is based on the money and greed we take for granted. What I'm saying is (and nobody wants to hear this) that the money grubbing, prideful motivation of our society must be addressed before any real change can occur. Our whole money, health, and food distribution within our evolved social systems must be changed to not just benefit a few but *to benefit everyone*. We have to bury the idea that our only *my* well-being is important in this interconnected cosmos, and we must work for the well-being of *everyone*. If we keep this distribution tool called money, we need for people to use their money not just for their own needs, but also for the rest of the world's population who don't have enough to live comfortably, or even survive.

In other words we should compassionately and peacefully support the equality and well-being of everyone and everything everywhere. We should stop being individualists and become egalitarian to treat all life on the Earth with equal kindness. We'd need to stop all militancy to stop our selfish fighting for our ideas, cultures and land. We'd need to see that all of us are one species and one family that are interconnected to this Earth and all life forms, and work together through one representative, democratic government, under the guidance of The Way, toward a new, helpful, sustainable evolution within the cosmos

I wish you all well on your journeys, but after reading this book, I hope you will have the courage to step out on your own and consider making this very exciting, powerful journey. I hope you'll join those who are turning away from the darkness of this present evolutionary state to discover the welcome truths that can help us get out and move on. I am sure that if others can journey with us, there still is hope for our species, because The Way awaits us, and The Way is the only way. It is the only way that can lead us out of ourselves and pride's dark despair to open to us a future. Come, let's journey within The Way together.

I'll close with some quotes from two of my favorite very wise people, the Islamist Jalal ad-Din Muhammad Rumi, and the Sanatani Hindu Mahatma Gandhi.

"Why do you stay in prison when the door
is so wide-open?
You wander from room to room hunting for the
diamond necklace that is already around your neck.
There is a candle in your heart ready to be kindled.
There is a void in your soul ready to be filled. You
feel it, don't you?
My soul is from elsewhere and I intend
to end up there.
I'm drenched in the flood which has yet to come. I'm
tied up in the prison which has yet to exist.
Love is the cure, for your pain will keep giving birth
to more pain until your eyes constantly exhale love
as effortlessly as your body yields its scent.
Love is not condescension, never that, nor books,
nor any marking on paper, nor what people say of
each other. Love is a tree with branches reaching for
eternity."
You were born with wings, why prefer to crawl
through life?
A voice inside the beat says, 'I know you're tired,
but come. This is the way." Rumi

"Anger is the enemy of non-violence,
and pride is a monster that swallows it up.
In a gentle way you can shake the world.
Morality is the basis of things, and truth is the
substance of morality.
An eye for an eye only ends up making
the whole world blind.
Nobody can hurt me without my permission.
The best way to find yourself

is to lose yourself in the service of others.
You must be the change you wish to see in the world.
The weak can never forgive. Forgiveness is the
attribute of the strong.
Strength does not come from physical capacity. It
comes from an indomitable will.
Live as if you were to die tomorrow. Learn as if you
were to live forever.
Happiness is when what you think, what you say and
what you do are in harmony.
The greatness of a nation can be judged by the way
its animals are treated.
Anger and intolerance are the enemies of correct
understanding.
It is health that is real wealth and not pieces of gold
or silver." Gandhi

Bon voyage my brave friends. A bright future awaits!

APPENDICES I

The Parliament of the World's Religions

In 1893, the city of Chicago hosted the World Columbian Exposition, an early world'sfair. So many people were coming to Chicago from all over the world that many smaller conferences,called Congresses and Parliaments, were scheduled to take advantage of this unprecedented gathering. One of these was the *World's Parliament of Religions,* an initiative of the Swedenborgian layman (and judge) Charles Carroll Bonney.The Parliament of Religions was by far the largest of the congresses held in conjunction with the Exposition. John Henry Barrows, a clergyman, was appointed as the first chairman of the General Committee of the 1893 Parliament by Charles Bonney.

The Parliament of Religions opened on 11 September 1893 at theWorld's Congress Auxiliary Building which is now The Art Institute of Chicago, and ran from 11 to 27 September, marking it the first organized interfaith gathering. Today it is recognized as the occasion of the birth of formal interreligious dialogue worldwide, with representatives of a wide variety of religions and new religious movements, including:

* The Jain preacher Virchand Gandhi was invited there as representative of Jainism.
* The Buddhist preacher Anagarika Dharmapala was invited there as a representative of Southern Buddhism," the term applied at that time to the Theravada.

- Soyen Shaku, the "First American Ancestor" of Zen, made the trip.
- An essay by the Japanese Pure Land master Kiyozawa Manshi, "Skeleton of the philosophy of religion" was read in his absence.
- Vivekananda represented India as a delegate, introducing Hinduism at the opening session of the Parliament on September 11.
- Islam was represented by Mohammed Alexander Russell Webb, an Anglo-American convert to Islam and the former US ambassador to Philippine.
- Rev. Henry Jessup addressing the World Parliament of Religions was the first to mention the Bahá'í Faith in the United States (it had previously been known in Europe. Since then Bahá'ís have become active participants.
- New religious movements of the time, such as Spiritualism and Christian Science. The latter was represented by Septimus J. Hanna, who read an address written by its founder Mary Baker Eddy.
- Absent from this event were Native American religious figures, Sikhs and other Indigenous and Earth centered religionists. It would not be until the 1993 Parliament that these religions and spiritual traditions would be represented.

From March to May 1930, Kyoto, Japan hosted a Great Religious Exposition. Shūkyō Dai-hakurankai. Religious groups from across Japan and China exhibited at the fair. All of Japan's traditional Buddhist sects had an exhibit, as well as Protestant and Catholic Christianity and the new religious sect Oomoto. The Oomoto pavilion, which included a mural of all the world's religions, hands-on pottery painting, and humorous paintings of Bodhidharma, attracted the most interest and coverage by far. Many visitors returned to the Oomoto pavilion, which was constantly being updated, six or seven times over the two months of the exposition.

In 1993, the Parliament convened at the Palmer House hotel in Chicago. Over 8,000 people from all over the world, from many diverse religions, gathered to celebrate, discuss and explore how religious traditions can work together on the critical issues which confront the world. A document, "Towards a Global Ethic: An Initial Declaration" (see ### below), mainly drafted by Hans Küng, set the tone for the subsequent ten days of discussion. This global ethic was endorsed by many of the attending religious and spiritual leaders who were part of the parliament assembly. Also created for the 1993 parliament was a book, *A Sourcebook for the Community of Religions*, by the late Joel Beversluis, which has become a standard textbook in religion classes. Unlike most textbooks of religion, each entry was written by members of the religion in question. The keynote address was given by the Dalai Lama on the closing day of the assembly. Cardinal Joseph Bernardin also participated.

More than 7,000 individuals from over 80 countries attended 1999 Parliament in Cape Town, South Africa. The Parliament began with a showing of the international AIDS Memorial Quilt to highlight the epidemic of AIDS in South Africa, and of the role that religious and spiritual traditions play in facing the critical issues that face the world. The event continued with hundreds of panels, symposia and workshops, offerings of prayer and meditation, plenaries and performances. The programs emphasized issues of religious, spiritual, and cultural identity, approaches to interreligious dialogue, and the role of religion in response to the critical issues facing the world today. The Parliament Assembly considered a document called *A Call to Our Guiding Institutions*, addressed to religion, government, business, education, and media inviting these institutions to reflect on and transform their roles at the threshold of the next century. In addition to the *Call*, the Parliament staff had created a book, *Gifts of Service to the World*, showcasing over 300 projects considered to be making a difference in the world. The Assembly members also deliberated about Gifts of Service which they could offer or could pledge to support among those projects gathered in the *Gifts* document.

Celebrated in the Universal Forum of Cultures, more than 8,900 individuals attended the 2004 Parliament in Barcelona, Spain. Having created the declaration *Towards a Global Ethic* at the 1993 Parliament and attempted to engage guiding institutions at the 1999 Parliament, the 2004 Parliament concentrated on four pressing issues: mitigating religiously motivated violence, access to safe water, the fate of refugees worldwide, and the elimination of external debt in developing countries. Those attending were asked to make a commitment to a "simple and profound act" to work on one of these issues.

Forum Monterrey 2007 was an international event which included Parliament-style events and dialogues. It was held as part of the 2007 Universal Forum of Cultures, which featured international congresses, dialogues, exhibitions, and spectacles on the themes of peace, diversity, sustainability and knowledge. Special emphasis was placed on the eight objectives of the Millennium Development goals for eradicating abject poverty around the world.

Melbourne, Australia, hosted the 2009 Parliament of the World's Religions. The 2009 parliament took place from 3 to 9 December. Over 6,000 people attended the parliament. It addressed issues of Aboriginal reconciliation. The issues of sustainability and global climate change were explored through the lens of indigenous spiritualities. Environmental issues and the spirituality of youth were also key areas of dialogue. The Council for a Parliament of the World's Religions suggested that the Melbourne parliament would "educate participants for global peace and justice" through exploring religious conflict and globalization, creating community and cross-cultural networks and addressing issues of religious violence. It supported "strengthening religious and spiritual communities" by providing a special focus on indigenous and Aboriginal spiritualities; facilitating cooperation between Pagan, Jewish, Christian, Bahá'í, Jain, Muslim, Buddhist, Sikh and Hindu communities; crafting new responses to religious extremism and confronting homegrown terrorism and violence.

In 2011, The Parliament of World's Religions announced that the 2014 Parliament would take place in Brussels, Belgium. In November 2012, a joint statement from Brussels and CPWR announced that because of the financial crisis in Europe, Brussels was unable to raise the funds required for a Parliament]

The 2015 The Parliament took place at the Salt Palace Convention Center in Salt Lake City, Utah. 9,806 attendees, performers, and volunteers from 73 countries, 30 Major Religions and 548 Sub-Traditions participated.

The Parliament of the World's Religions 1993 drafted a statement written initially by Dr. Hans Kung in cooperation with

CPWR staff and Trustees and experts drawing on many of the world's religious and spiritual traditions. It was called **Towards a Global Ethic**. This declaration identified four essential, shared affirmations that were essential to a global ethic..It Affirmed respect for all life, economic justice and solidarity, tolerance, truthfulness, equal rights and partnership between men and women. The document elaborated eloquently on the significance of each value for our modern world, and was endorsed by the 1993 Parliament of the World's Religions in Chicago, USA. Towards a Global Ethic urges all men and women of good will to join in a commitment to these vital, shared principles. It's become quite famous and has been used throughout the world by universities, religious, spiritual communities and interfaith organizations, Towards a Global Ethic has emerged as one of the most significant building blocks in the continuing process of creating global ethical understanding and consensus, and I believe that it could be the **best reference to The Way that has thus far been drafted.**

APPENDICES II

The Evolution of Humans

Early Hominoids

The evolution from the Southern ape of Africa to humans came amazingly fast in evolutionary terms. As I'm sure you know, your closest animal relatives would have also been the closest relatives of the modern chimpanzee and ape. Chimpanzees share 98% of your genes. They can hold grudges, nurse resentments, form strong family ties, and experience grief over the loss of a loved one. They can also learn simple mathematical skills and recognize themselves in a mirror. But of course, you did not *come from* modern monkeys or apes, as many of your books report. You simply share their ancient ancestors.

Your earliest human ancestor, *Australopithecus Africans* (the "southern ape of Africa") lived three million years ago. They have been termed *Homo habilis* (The handy human because they could use stone tools). They had a slightly larger brain than modern chimpanzees but had very limited communication skills. They also had a limited ability to look ahead or plan for a hunt. They had only a limited ability for mental abstraction. The potential for your modern human consciousness was present but very latent, waiting to unfold those three million years ago.

Homo habilis then evolved into *Homo erectus* (the upright human) 1.5 million years ago. Their super-complex brain capacity had jumped (in 2.5 million years) over 450 cubic centimeters. It was this being with a jutting brow, low forehead, and massive jaw that made the journey from Africa to the cooler climates of Europe and Asia. Dealing with an ice age, they learned to develop warm clothing, build tents for shelters, and hunt with a new level of proficiency. Inventiveness and social cooperation grew, so that 500,000 years ago they developed a way to control fire, though they could not, as of yet, start one. Using a few words, hand gestures, and dramatic facial expression they began a more sophisticated communication. They were not violent beings. Instead, they sought cooperation over competition. (Humanities potential for violence apparently did not blossom until much later.)

The origin of what is called *modern humans or Homo sapiens* is hotly debated. Some feel that they appeared in Africa as recently as 200,000 years ago, and quickly spread around the world to replace all other evolved human groupings. Others feel that they first appeared in Africa over a million years ago and then developed into modern humans in several separate regions around the world. But however it occurred, the transition from *Homo erectus* to *Homo sapiens* (the wise human) marks a dramatic jump in reflective consciousness.

This dramatic change can be observed in the earliest *Homo sapiens,* who were called *Neanderthals*. Though they began around 200,000 years ago, they suddenly became extinct around 35,000 years ago. They had a large brain capacity although they did not have your modern anatomical form.

You are directly descended from another type of *Homo sapiens* who is often called *Cro-Magnon* (taken from the place in France where they were first found). No one knows why the Neanderthal vanished and the Cro-Magnon flourished. One theory indicates that the Cro-Magnon was more adaptive. Other theories say the Cro-Magnon killed off the Neanderthal. Another says that they died off from a greater vulnerability to disease. Still another says that they were absorbed by the more superior Cro-Magnon through interbreeding. Whatever happened, 35,000 years ago the world became inhabited exclusively by a physically modern humans called **Homo sapiens sapiens** (doubly wise human) who have swarmed, dominated and, recently destroyed the Earth.

Hunter-gatherers

Homo sapiens sapiens evolution began with the early *hunter-gatherers* (35,000 to 15,000 B.C.) who lived off of animals, nuts and berries and were clearly able to step back and observe themselves. They saw the world as being alive with magical and mysterious forces that were used to explain it all. Their social organization and identity came from their affiliation with their tribe (an extended family). Their aesthetic side is manifested in the presence of jewelry and ornaments, as well as their primitive cave art that consisted of drawn animals and signs with dots, grids and zigzags. They lived at one with nature. The author Duane Elgin talks about a *"two dimensional" consciousness* with a compressed mixture of instincts, bodily sensations, emotions and loosely formed concepts. Life was basically unexamined and taken for granted. Their responses were generally habitual and instinctual.

Around 15,000 to 8,000 B.C. we find the amazing period of cave art, which emanated from the final five thousand years of an ice age. 80% of known cave art came from that time. In it was found sophisticated and exuberant expressions of animals, but it provided only crude stick figures for humans. (This could indicate that they had too little reflective consciousness to draw detail at this stage, or it could indicate a taboo against painting the human face or form.)

We also find a primitive travel network developing. Rather than economic exchanges, these networks are thought to have reflected social exchanges that built relationships and avoided conflicts. They definitely began an expanded sense of community that extended out for many miles.

Domestication and Agrarian Culture

It can be no accident that the hunter-gatherers way of life ended with the close of an ice age. As glaciers retreated, the weather became warmer and more humid. Gradually, forests replaced grasslands. A change of consciousness was coming into being as we find experiments in the planting of seeds and the domestication of animals.

Old faceless and primitive Earth Goddess figurines (which first appeared around 26,000 B.C.) had detailed faces and striking eyes made of inlaid stone. (This increase in the details of the human form seems to parallel the move into an *agrarian culture*.) A new self-awareness was afoot. In this next stage in the evolution of consciousness, which Elgin calls *depth consciousness*, humans were able to stand back from nature and recognize within it cycles and seasons.

With the advent of deliberate farming and a resulting small-village way of life, the first *large scale agrarian-based civilizations emerged* beginning around 3500 B.C. in Mesopotamia. These people have been called the "Sumerians," and from them, Babylon emerged. However, Egypt (2800 B.C.), as well as Stonehenge in England (2800 B.C.), India (2500 B.C.), China 1500 B.C.), and Mexico (1200 B.C.) followed with agrarian city/states shortly thereafter. These agrarian and celestially oriented civilizations blossomed all over the world at roughly the same time. Their shift from a nomadic way of life dramatically altered the entire social, religious, economic, and moral order.

In these first *city/state civilizations*, the wonders of making the incredible wheel, writing, mathematics, astronomy, irrigation, government, armies, architecture, metal technology, pottery, weaving and organized religion suddenly exploded into their consciousness. All of these civilizations bustled with life and trade.

Not long after the emergence of armies, the peaceful evolution of humanity disappeared. Wars for territory, influence and the prestige of rulers caused empires to rise and fall with great frequency and regularity. Eventually, wars were not defensive acts at all. The subjugation of others became an accepted, and even honored, vocation within the culture.

As the agrarian culture grew, there was a shift from a plant and animal centered "Earth Goddess" religion to a "Sky God" heaven and star centered orientation. Humanity began to look up.

Out of this came a priestly class that continued into the Middle Ages. Essentially every known civilization – except (for a brief time) the Greek/Roman one – took its spiritual instruction from *priestly watchers of the sky.* These professional full-time priests got their authority from observing and interpreting the skies. These observations quickly altered their perception of time. As they looked up, they began to see seasons, cycles, and the rhythms of nature. They came to know when to plant, cultivate and harvest crops. As had the entrails of animals in the previous age, so now the sky was used to tell the future.

The old egalitarian social structure evolved into a culture reflecting distinctly different social classes like kings, merchants, soldiers, peasants, and artisans. Their society lost the focus on the value and good of everyone and focused on the wealth and power of a few. The priests had the greatest authority since they claimed their authority from above. Increasingly powerful sky gods were lifted up to advance the priests wealth and power.

Most of the people were peasant farmers who paid little attention to the rise and fall of their increasingly powerful leadership. Their interests lay in their crops. There was no middle class, which meant that almost everything rested on the peasant's shoulders.

It should be said that within the early civilizations, there was no significant past or future reflection. Although they developed primitive writing techniques, they recorded no history. None of these civilizations possessed the intellectual tools for historical evaluation or interpretation.

In some ways, even though there was some new emotional bonding that came out of the myth that they could own land, there was much more violence that resulted from this in the galloping growth of group pride. It was manifested in the militarism and war that was needed to defend their land and property. This meant that their identification was no longer rooted in nature, but became rooted in their newly formed city/states and their prideful cultures.

The Classical Age, the Dark Ages and the Renaissance

Around 600 BC, there was a new shift in human consciousness. An explosion of reflection appeared in the new civilizations in Greece, Persia, Rome, China, and India. Great leaps in philosophy, religion, art, science and government were found in all of these cultures. As the concept of history (written down evolution) arrived and some limited literacy grew, events began to be recorded in all of these locations. Great cultures emerged in the Middle East, Greece and Rome, developing the Jewish religion, Greek philosophy, and the durable Roman Empire). Equal contributions came from the Byzantium and Muslim cultures, together with China, India and the Americas (where the Mayan empire reached its height around 800 AD and then fell into decline).

By 500 AD the Roman Empire collapsed in the West, resulting in what is termed "The Dark Ages". But in the East, the Byzantium Empire (located in Mediterranean Asia) continued the spark of learning and culture for another thousand years. Around 1100 AD, both the Crusades and the amazing compass facilitated massive and more sophisticated travel. Europe's touching of the booming Byzantium Empire with its advanced civilization is believed by many to have awakened the West out of its Dark Ages.

Around 1500 AD, the famous "Renaissance" came to Europe re-establishing the arts and sciences and bringing a needed reformation to the powerful religious structures. Thus the leadership in the advance of civilization shifted from Asia and Africa to the West. Voyages to the Americas (mainly by the Spanish) resulted in the tragic destruction of the vibrant civilizations in Central America and North America. Greed and power took over as England, Europe and North America drifted into the exploitation of slavery.

The Scientific/Industrial Era with its Many Revolutions

By the late 1700s Science with its application in industry, lead to a giant revolution in England and most of Europe. Within the scope of a mere three hundred years, an entirely new approach to life with a totally new identity emerged.

All of this began with sweeping changes associated with *several revolutions*. For instance, the **Scientific Revolution** totally transformed the way you looked at yourselves and the world. (The discovery of the cosmos with it endless mass and stars opened us to how minuscule and we are, and recently made it clear that our reflective species is not alone. It opened to us natural laws that are discernible through reason. It also challenged the literal interpretation of many religious myths that lead to another reformation – the **Religious Reformation.** Following the renaissance, people began to question many of the superstitions that had evolved into the religions. Abuse of power in the leadership of the Church was brought into question that later brought into question the divine right of kings and queens. This instigated a new secular search for government based on the rights of all the people.

And of course the most publicized was the **Industrial Revolution.** Old Human and animal energy were replaced by the power of coal, natural gas, gasoline and the resulting electricity. The steam engine allowed for the mechanization of fields and factories. Trade barriers were opened up as money overtook bartering, and money became widely available and ultimately to goal of industrialized societies. All of this resulted in an availability of unprecedented wealth, but mainly to the rich and powerful.

A different kind of **Agricultural Revolution** emerged from the improvements in the technology of planting, cultivating, transporting and storing food. Productivity soared, meeting the needs of an increased population (which has now gone crazy) and allowing vast numbers of people to survive in the growing urban environments.

An **Urban Revolution** paralleled the rise of Industry as people swarmed into cities to get work in industry. Great cities arose from the steady flow of people moving away from the country to get new jobs. Slowly, a small part of the impoverished peasant class began to form a new middle class.

And all of this created a **Democratic Revolution.** There was a change in the meaning of the word "freedom" to not just mean the empowerment of the landed gentry or merchants, but everyone. It especially empowered the middle class with a new availability of education. The power and respect for kings and queens, dukes and earls, and all other people of title, shrank before the growing respect for the rights of everyone before the law. This revolution began in Europe, expanded greatly in North America, and eventually moved out to transform the world.

The New Reality

Up until this period of incredible change, reality had fit into a very small box. But with the rapid revelations of science and the rise of literacy and education, a dramatic change occurred:

Evolution, anthropology and paleontology kicked out one wall of your small box of *time*. The perception of the beginning of things went from 4000 years ago to many billions of years ago. The end of time went from something that could arrive any moment to something wide open to speculation.

Size was the next to go. With the invention of the *microscope*, the infinitesimal came into view. With the *telescope,* the vastness of our solar system, and ultimately the cosmos, burst into view.

The wonders of life and human development were opened up by new disciplines of biology and anthropology.

The complicated *foundation of things* was addressed by chemistry, physics and mathematics.

The *interactions of people and groups* were discussed by psychology and sociology.

Actually, such vast discoveries over such a short period of time caused many people to be disoriented and giddy as they stood before such a vast display of information. . Education grew from being something for the very few into something that was necessary for everyone. It became necessary in order to survive in such a vastly altered and complicated world.

The full impact of all of the industrial activity did not occur until the 1900s. Many things dramatically changed our world, such as the steam engine in 1765 that powered locomotives, boats and factories; and also the McCormick reaper in the mid-1800s that revolutionized mass harvesting techniques. But nothing can overemphasize the impact of the gasoline-powered automobiles and airplanes together with the general use of electricity, light bulbs, and telephones (to name only a few). As of now there is both excitement and confusion about the world wide explosion of computers. All of these things have transformed every aspect of our life.

By the 1960s, industrial societies had radio, television, the nuclear bomb, and the jet engines. You also had suburban cultures, with their serious outbreaks of depression (where psychiatrists abounded).

1969 saw people on the moon. (Seeing the earth from the moon gave people another new perspective.) The first Earth Day was in 1970 fueling the realization that we might be a species that was doubling its population over 7 times in the 1900s and thus killing off the plants and animals who came before us, and ourselves as well. The global communications revolution also appeared in the 1990s, followed by a global economy and a new, limited, global spirituality, and both excitement and confusion over the world wide explosion of computers.

It is a strange fact that after our *200 thousand* years of evolution, things have happened to bring about our species extinction in just *1 hundred* years. At the turn of the 20th century, population grew from 1 billion to 7 billion to tragically over-populate the world and wipe out the delicate balance of the Earth's ecosystems. Also industrialization using cheep fuel polluted the air, the need for more food polluted the land, oceans, and waterways, we cut the number of animals in half, used up the fresh water, and depleted to almost nothing the fish and other sea-life. Our deforestation, to clear land for residences and then get wood to build them, dropped our oxygen level just as industrialization was causing a lot more CO2 to enter the atmosphere. This last stage of this evolution is no doubt the last stage in the evolution of our species..

APPENDICES III

A. *The Evolution of Recent Human Religions*

Part I. The Evolution of Some of the Religions of the Western World

It has been said that there are over 6000 ongoing religions presently existing in the world, each of which has countless branches or sects. We can obviously only look at and reflect on a few of them. I'll begin by looking at those that may well be the most familiar to most of us.

(Much of this you will already have read in the section on religions from "How Things Can Help Us Recognize The Way". Don't get upset; just skip it if you want to and read on. Thank you.)

Judaism

Much of Jewish, Christian and Islamic history begins back in Babylon where we find a set of loosely knit nomads called Habiru. Around 1900 BC, there was a great migration of these people from around the Persian Gulf across the Fertile Crescent. Genesis (in the scriptures of the Abrahamic Faiths) tells us that a clan leader named Abraham moved out of Ur because of a call from El- Shaddai (the God of the Mountains). He moved away from a land of many gods to a land where Abraham and his descendants were to worship this specific God. It was all sealed in a covenant.

In truth, El -Shaddai was still just one of the many clan gods. (The book of Genesis was written much later.) The concept of the one God for the whole world was involved a long process of evolution that moved throughout Jewish Scripture and was recently still evolving in many of the living religions. In other words, seeing one God as existing just for me, or for my group or nation, was still very much alive.

It was around 1285 BC that another powerful Jewish leader emerged. Moses was able to instill in an enslaved people a sense of unity and identity that centered on a God he called "Yahweh". Once again, the events of this people's origin were recorded much later, and the myths that evolved around these events have defined the Jewish people up to this day.

However, the Yahweh that Moses worshiped was still not seen as the one and only God of all the nations, rather, it was the national God of the newly united Israelite tribes. Moses can thus be seen as another step up the ladder from Mesopotamian and Egyptian polytheism. There was still a long way to go to reach monotheism. We see this addressed in the Jewish prophets, the wisdom literature, and most especially during the Babylonian Exile (that lasted from 587 to 536 B.C). But, so powerfully did the concept of the one God for the Jewish people eventually evolve that when they were taken over by the Greeks, and later the Romans, they refused to give up that which had become so central to their belief - the one God, Yahweh.

To the Torah, were added the Tanach and Talmud influences. They were all interpreted in vastly different ways by the different branches of Judaism. At last count, there were about 14 million Jews (about .22% of those who professed a religion worldwide – a small number compared to their huge impact) worshiping in their Synagogues.

Christianity

A Jewish man from Galilee, whose birth and early childhood remains covered in myth, appeared at the Jordan River where a Jewish prophet (known as John the Baptizer) was preaching repentance and a return to the observance of the Jewish covenant. After a time with John, Jesus himself was baptized and separated from John to move on in a different direction in his reformation of Judaism.

Rather than judgment, he preached forgiveness. Rather than a strict adherence to Jewish law, he taught an adherence to the God of justice, compassion, and love revealed in much of Jewish scripture, especially in the prophets.

Though he remained out in the country, his great success in forming an all-inclusive healing community of followers began to threaten the religious establishment in the city of Jerusalem. Because his teachings were seen as radical in his attempt to bring about a reformation of peace and justice, and because of an incident in the Temple during the Jewish Passover where he was repulsed by the greed that pervaded the worship, the occupying Romans, with the support of the Jewish Sanhedrin, crucified him.

Though it was clear that he had no intention of forming another religion (he was clearly a Jewish reformer), the myths spread, the organizations grew, and the Christian religion emerged. Evolving myth first brought Jesus into an identification with the messiah of Jewish mythology, and it even opened the way for Jesus to be seen as being a part of God. The Zoroastrian dualism of a heaven and a hell (as well as the envisioning of a devil as the opposite of God) soon evolved into the religion. Myths evolved professing Jesus (now called the "Christ", which means "messiah" in Greek) to be the sacrifice God had made for "Christians" (the followers of Jesus, which later came to be known as the "Church") for their sins. Along with this grew the myth allowing anyone who identified with Christianity to in some way go to a place called "heaven" after death.

Christianity's evolution was a bumpy one. Jesus original teachings were recorded far after his death and were thus altered to reflect the already evolving massive myths. They were also often altered in translation to further reflect these myths (either on purpose or by mistake).

Eventually, his original teachings were ignored amidst all the superstition and politics that ensued. However, inspirational leaders and reformers within the faith have always seemed to manage to keep some of his original teachings and ideas alive. In fact some followers believed that the impact of those teachings on the world lifted the spiritual and humanitarian mindset of humanity so profoundly that it offered hope for humanity's journey toward unity and peace.

Christians adhered to a slightly amended version of the Jewish scriptures plus what came to be called <u>The New Testament.</u> Churches interpreted these scriptures in different ways. There recently were about 2.1 billion Christians in the world (about 33% of those who professed a religion) though their numbers were in the process of dropping.

Islam

Islam, coming from the word "Salaam" (meaning peace or surrender) emerged in the hot, barren desert of Saudi Arabia in 622 AD to a people whose ancient polytheistic religion was in the process of dying. Their lives had been subject to the fate of desert jinns (spirits), marauding desert Bedouins, the whims of a brutal ruling class, and the exploitation of corrupt merchants. Centuries of contact with Judaism and Christianity in the Near East, Egypt, and North Africa (which were sometimes friendly and sometimes not), had familiarized them with the concept of one God. However, Islam evolved to be as different from Judaism and Christianity, just as Christianity evolved to be different from Judaism. Having said this, I would point out that they all saw themselves as descendants of Abraham (using much of the same scripture), and Islam believed that both Moses and Jesus were great prophets.

Islam believed that Mohamed was the last and greatest of all the prophets. They believed that he brought the message of enlightenment from the Angel Gabriel that was recorded in the Koran. Out of the peoples polytheistic past, the prophet Mohamed preached of Allah, the one God, who spoke to his people through his prophet. He called them to a new way of life and a new way of looking at religion.

Contrary to our knowledge of Jesus, we know that Mohamed was born in 571 AD in Mecca. Both his parents died when he was a child. He was cared for by his grandfather and then by an uncle. He worked as a shepherd and later, as a caravan worker organizing caravan trips. In spite of the horrible corruption and graft around him, he was known as an upright and trustworthy man. At 25, he was hired by a wealthy widow to manage her affairs. Later they were married. She loved and assisted him throughout his life and mission.

Troubled by the horrible conditions around him, Mohamed took time off from his work for over 15 years to go to a cave close to Mecca. There he would pray and ask for solutions to the problems that were destroying his people. He developed a relationship with Allah, the name of one of the spirits of his countrymen. He became convinced that Allah was neither a spirit nor just another God, but was what his name claimed: the one God. Soon the famous phrase, which was to unify and rally a divided and burdened people, rang out through the entire world "La Ilaha Illa Allah!" (There is no God but Allah). Mohamed preached his message to free the people of Mecca from their ignorance and superstition, and from their bondage to immorality.

The myth is that in the cave a voice came to him three times saying, "recite." Then, the angel Gabriel is said to have dictated the Qumran to him. Mohamed spent the rest of his life in an uncompromising and unrelenting effort to bring the message of Allah to all of his people.

He made it clear that he could work no wonders and was only a preacher. He suffered, as did Moses and Jesus, great persecution, ridicule and humiliation. He was cutting into the revenues paid to the shrines and temples of the many spirits. He was also preaching that all people were equal which threatened the rigid social structure; and his strict moral code threatened the multitude of degradations that infested the people.

He had to leave Mecca for Medina. This "hegira" (flight) in 622 A.D. is the Islamic point for determining their dates. After 3 years he had less than 40 followers. However, after 10 years he had won over 5,000 people to his cause. Gradually, not only did he become a preacher, leader, and politician, but in self-defense, he became a warrior as well – all in the name of Allah. Upon his death in 632 A.D., essentially all of Arabia was under his control. One hundred years later Muslims, with their 5 principals (or obligations) imposed by the Koran, controlled much of the civilized world.

The Qur'an and Hadith have been interpreted literally for over 1300 years, and has become the fastest growing religion in the world.

About 1.5 billion followers gather in their Mosques (about 21% of the world's believers).

Part II. The Evolution of Some of the Religions of the Eastern World

Hinduism

Whereas the fundamentalism of Islam served to block its natural evolution of thought, ***Hinduism*** (the most ancient of the living religions) possessed an openness of mind that allowed it to accept new ideas and truths (thus also making it one of the most modern). To the Hindu, ultimate reality was unknowable. They believed that humans were incapable of knowing any absolute truth. Thus, they *accepted all religions* that were open to the struggle for meaning. For them, the ultimate reality, or "Brahman", was the ground of *all* being.

The many invasions of **India** only served to contribute to this amazing complexity. They always had the ability to see the religions of their conquerors as some further expression of their own. Basically, they believed in Brahman the creator, Vishnu the preserver, Shiva the destroyer, or any other of a great pantheon of Gods (said to approach 33 million).

Around these Gods, ancient myths going back to the hunter/ gathers grew and developed. These myths were accepted as an attempt to understand the different aspects of Brahman. Of course, Hinduism, as was true of all religions, was mired in its own complex cacophony of superstitions with its miracles, magic, pantheism and reincarnation.

Hindus do not feel that they belong to a religion; in fact, each interprets Hinduism in his or her own way. There are no boundaries. Hinduism is thus a subtly unified conglomerate of ancient mythologies, yogic disciplines, meditations and evolving speculations. As we said, it is one of the expressions of the very beginnings of religious evolution, while also being one of the expressions of modern life.

The very new and the very old have found space within its flexible inclusiveness. There is no recorded founder of Hinduism because its history fades into its timeless past.

Especially interesting to me is the Hindu concept of the person. It is seen as the expression of a reservoir of being that never dies, an infinite center, and a hidden presence that is often referred to as "Atman". He is the world's soul from which all souls come and to which all souls return. This hidden center in everything is also seen as a part of Brahman.

But they have believed that instead of humans identifying with their innermost soul, they choose to identify with a surface-self. To throw off this preoccupation with the illusion of the surface and attain union with their deepest divine-selves (called Nirvana), Hinduism developed various elaborate systems, or paths, to follow in approaching Nirvana.

They also developed a strong belief in reincarnation and Karma. This meant that one's future depended on the living of a good life, which then determined the quality of their next incarnation. The life, in which one was stuck at any given time, was called one's Karma. The fixed caste system of India went back thousands of years, and, where a person might fit into that caste system was called their Karma.

The Bhagavad-Gita, Upanishads, and Rig Veda make up some of the scripture that is commonly used in this multi-layered, complex religion. There are about 900 million people who gather in their Mandirs, Mandiras, and Temples to make up about 14% of the world's believers.

Buddhism

As was true of Jesus of Nazareth, so it was true of Siddhartha Gautama, or as he later became known, *The Buddha* (563 to 486 BC). His intention was also not to start another religion. He just wanted to reform Hinduism from its superstitions and dehumanizing practices.

He was raised as a Hindu and enjoyed the benefits of being the son of a very wealthy Sakya clan Chief. His protected life was shocked when he discovered the poverty, disease and suffering of his people. Following his association with a holy man, he set out to follow a similar path. At the age of 35, he became *a* buddha. (To be called *a* buddha was recognition of having reached enlightenment. There were many men who were recognized as buddhas, but only Gautama was ever called *the* Buddha.)

He rejected some of Hinduism such as: the caste system, the concept of many Gods, and the need to go through many rebirths (which had caused a total submission to one's fate). He went out to teach what he called "The Middle Way" that taught love, forgiveness and peace and outlined and refined the practice of meditation From his influence there evolved Four Sacred and Noble Truths, the last of which was to follow the Eight-fold Path to Perfection (which involved the destruction of desire).

He gathered many disciples and spent the next 45 years in Northeastern India spreading his word. Like Jesus, he insisted that he was no more than a humble servant of the people, and that he was certainly not endowed with any unusual powers. However, after his death at Kushinagara when he was 85 years of age, myths began to spread. As with Jesus, He came to be looked upon as a God by his followers. In spite of what he wished, he too ended up being the founder of another one of the world's great religions.

As is true with all religions, when Buddhism spread, it took on a multitude of different forms. Surprisingly, it did not become the dominant religion of India, although it ultimately became the dominant religion of China. (This is thought to have happened because its radical reforms were never really accepted in India.)

The Tripitake and Sutras were the common texts of its 376 million adherents. They met in Pagodas, Stupas, and Temples to make up about 6% of the world's believers.

Sikhism

Sikhism (from "Sikh" meaning student or disciple) was a religion founded in 1507 A.D. that came out of Punjab (which ended up as a part of northern India). It was not well known in the West, but it was one of the world's largest religions. Most adherents lived in the Punjab region, but they also spread out across much of the world. It was founded on the teachings of the 10 Gurus (meaning teachers or mentors). Nanak was the first Guru and was thus identified as Sikhism's founder.

Sikhism believed in Vahiguru, the all-powerful God. They advocated the pursuit of salvation using disciplined personal meditation on the name and message of Vahiguru. They abhorred any anthropomorphic interpretations of Vahiguru; in fact they were actually open to the interpretation of Vahiguru as being the cosmos.

The Sikhs followed the teachings of the 10 Gurus, as well as their scripture called Guru Granth Sahib (which was decreed by the tenth Guru but really included the selected works of many of its followers). Though there was much about the traditions, history and culture of the Punjab region in their scripture, there was much more about the equality of all humanity (including a rejection of the caste system) that led them to welcome people of all nationalities and religions into their faith. They also believed in the living of a responsible, involved life. The goal of life was to move from Manmukh (self-centeredness) to Gurmukh (God-centeredness). This included the qualities of humility, selfless service, and openly adhering to the teaching of the Gurus.

The Sikhs faced persecution from some Hindus and even at times from the Indian Government. This was exemplified in a famous raid by Indira Gandhi on their center of worship, called the Golden Temple. This act led them into a reluctant militarism that later tarnished their reputation. Like the Tibetan Buddhists in China, they longed for their freedom and independence from India so they could live out their lives in peace. Sikhism has 23 million members.

The Religions of China

Until the early 20th century, China was ruled by a succession of Emperors (seen as Gods) and dynasties going back over 5,000 years. Isolated by their topography, they developed a highly sophisticated system of agriculture, economics, government, art, architecture, and engineering. Though a unique form of *Buddhism* has more recently dominated the religious landscape of China, *Confucianism* and *Taoism* continued to remain influential and were unique to China.

The Chinese always felt that all of life had a pattern. They came to believe in the eternal interplay between *yang and yin*. Yang was a term that generally referred to an active, forceful principal, while yin referred to a receptive, flexible principal. The interplay between the two (active-receptive) is what they felt produced everything . Male/female, water/its container, sound/silence, big/small, light/darkness, life/death, and on and on).

These two opposites (yang and yin) were seen as forever pursuing each other in a harmonious circle and symbolized the way life should be lived. The art of living was to combine the yang and yin into a gentle balance. In this way, two of *China's indigenous religions followed the yang and the yin* in Confucianism stressing tradition while Taoism stressing spontaneity. Confucianism was mainly rational while Taoism was intuitive. Confucianism was more active while Taoism was more passive I will address these two of China's religions

Confucianism

Confucius or "Kung-Fu-tzu" (meaning "Kung The Teacher") was born around 551 BC. He grew up in poverty and knew well the sufferings of the people. At 15, he became a serious student and an expert in Chinese traditions. In his 20's he became a tutor, and his reputation as an honest and wise man began to spread. When he died in 479 BC, his teachings and writings had edited the best of Chinese tradition into a systematic teaching on wisdom. He grew in influence through a growing number of disciples.

Eventually, he became a household word, and his sayings became accepted as proverbs. In a time of horrific conflict, "Kung The Teacher" offered lessons that helped to restore order to the nation. They were based around the five principals of *Jen, Chun-tzu, Li, Te,* and *Wen*. It is said that this religion was the fist of the many religions to say that we should approach and treat other people as ourselves.

Confucianism had about 6.3 million followers using the <u>Lun Yu</u> as their scripture in their Temples, Shrines, and Seowons.

Taoism

Tao (pronounced "Dow") means path or way. As Confucius spoke of the way life *ought* to be, so Lao Tzu (meaning the grand old teacher) gave equal weight to the way life really *is*. Lao Tzu (who many believe to be a legendary figure) wrote the <u>Tao te Ching</u> (meaning "The Way and its Power").

Taoism soon split into three branches: *Popular superstition* leaning on magic and sorcery; *a complicated form of mystical thinking*; and a *philosophy of the natural way* (nature's way) in which things work themselves out.

It is in this last form that influenced just about everything in Chinese culture. Recently, it had even begun to have some influence on western culture. The expressions "go with the flow" and "if it ain't broke, don't fix it" came out of Taoism.

Taoism had about 2.7 million adherents. The Chinese traditional religions made up 6% of the world's religions.

The Religions of Japan

Any discussion of the religions of Japan must be a complicated one. *Christianity* from the West and *Buddhism* from China both had a huge impact on Japan. However, **Shintoism** (*Shin tao* meaning "the way of the Gods"), with its great stress on ancestors and tradition, was distinctly Japanese.

A belief called *Animatism*, which saw a spirit or a God in everything, was also unique to Japan. It is because of Animatism that the worship of nature remained a part of all Japanese worship.

Many resources say that the largest religion in Japan was *Shinto/Buddhist*, which was a unique combination both. Though Shintoism was listed as having between 2 to 4 million members world wide, such numbers remained confusing due to the extent of Japan's religious syncretism.

Part III. Some Other Recent Religions

I must at least mention some other religions that have had large numbers. For instance, different tribal religions, such as **Shamanism and Animism,** have had 232 million adherents (4% of world religions); **Juche** 19 million; **Spiritism** 15 million; **Bahai** 7 million; **Cao Dai** 4 million; **Zoroastrianism** 2.6 million; **Tenrikyo** 2 million; the **Unitarian Universal** movement, around 1 million; and of course professed **Atheists** (who deny any God or any need for a religion) 150 million. Atheists are different from those who claimed to have **no specific religious preference.** They stand at 775 million or 12%. One of my recent interests, because it affirms the wonder of the Earth, is **Noe-pantheism** whose numbers are unknown.

Some say it is appropriate to identify **Science** as a religion. It too has had its myths, legends and powerful leaders. It has also had a great number of dedicated and committed followers. Still, I would personally not classify Science as a religion. It clarifies and codifies empirical data relating to what can be presently understood. Conversely, I feel that religion recognizes, and dares to reach out into, the vast vistas of the unknown in the search of truth. It affirms that which is still mystery.

We have looked at a few representatives of the major Western and Eastern world religions, but they can be subdivided into about 270 large and influential religious groupings. They all attest to the thousands upon thousands of the Homo sapiens sapiens' different belief systems. For example, Christianity alone has been said to have 34,000 separate groupings. Thus any further study would not serve our purpose of opening up our understanding of the rich diversity of the Homo sapiens specie's religious evolution. We've got to stop somewhere

B. *My Opinion on the Subject of a Divine Being*

I have often been asked about the subject of what I've have always called "God", so I'll briefly address it here. Let me say that my opinion on this has no more value than yours because no one can speak definitively about any divine being. In every religion where this subject is addressed (and some do not address it), it is recognized that their God is immortal, eternal, and mysterious.

However I believe that in our species pride we still give our various Gods human, anthropomorphic, attributes. For instance, in the majority of religions, their Gods are identified as a male and called "Him". Gods are also called "Kings" who powerfully rule over the Earth. Gods are said to pick certain groups of people as their own and bestow upon these people might in battle and great wealth. They sometimes are said to be jealous of other Gods and they punish "his people" when they worship another God. It is commonly accepted that we can not only speak to their Gods, and that we have to do so in a specific language (seen as God's language). It is also thought that when we speak to a God, he will do as we say. Some religions say that that their God will not only hear but also answer prayers if a prayer comes from a member of their that religion, or do certain things like sacrificing some form of life, regularly attend worship services, pray at certain times in certain ways, are not divorced or gay or someone who drinks alcohol, plays cards or pool.. All of this seems to me to have taken the practice of making our Gods human into an insane extreme..

If you are about to discount me because I don't believe in your perception of God, let me say that when I look at who we are in relation to the cosmos (as well as subatomic theory), I do not see where there can be one, superior, human-like entity up in the sky ruling over everything. However I do see that we are a part of our amazing bodies with their billions of cells made up of countless numbers of molecules,,atoms, electrons, protons, neutrons and on and on.. I also see that we are a part of this amazing Earth with its complex life-support ecosystems, the Sun (our star) with its planets, all of the other billions of stars with their trillions of planets in our galaxy, all of the billions of galaxies that make up this gigantic cosmos, and a lot more that is so far beyond that we can't possibly know anything about it . For ;instance, there is so much about us that we will never understand like the things that are beyond the cosmos to be so far beyond our mental reach that we can't even begin to think about them. (Subatomic studies have said that there are other universes.and maybe even parallel universes.)

Of course I know that most people still believe that there is one presence out there that is behind, and in control of, everything. For me, thinking that way comes from a time that we should long ago have evolved beyond. For instance I think it comes from a time when nations were ruled by one dictator (like a king or queen), whereas now we know that democracy (the rule of everyone) works the best.. It comes from a time when dragons, sea-monsters, sorcerers, elves, fairies, witches, warlocks, readers of stars and dreams, and a hoist of other imagined things that at one time were accepted, But isn't it past time for us to cast these and other superstitions out, and with all of the new knowledge now have before us, move on?

Is there something that we can't now understand that is the source of everything and keeps it going? Could it be something that is beyond the cosmos and beyond our perception? I believe nothing can be ruled out because we are a new, just developing reflective spot in the cosmos, so we are surrounded by mystery. However I also think that we must be very careful to avoid swallowing, anthropomorphic, superstitious conclusions. We can't even assume that there is a beginning or an end to everything just because that's the way it is with us, and we can't assume that something is in control of everything for the same reason. For instance, I think it might be possible that everything is created and sustained by everything else in much the same way that the ecosystems of the Earth sustain themselves...or in the way that the cosmos, with its coming and going of stars, sustains itself. That may sound strange, but to me it makes more sense than the presence of some king-like being ruling over everything somewhere up in he sky.

As I've said before, I consider myself to be a mystic and a spiritual person. I live in humble wonder and awe before the complexity of all of life, the amazing beauty and nurture of the Earth, and the vast unknowable cosmos that is unfolding to us more and more everyday. I have many spiritual moments as I read, experience and evolve in my humanness. My seeing, hearing, smelling, and touching never cease to launch me into spiritual wonders that allow me to evolve into someone new and ever more grateful. I have found that searching for The Way has been a very spiritual thing, along with things like living, growing in knowledge, interacting with the Earth and its life forms, and even dying (as we go on in both the memory of loved ones and in having participated in and affected evolution's advance). In fact I see all being as spiritual since it is natural, mystical, and even somehow divine..

APPENDICES IV

Evolution

Evolution is a relatively new discovery. It began when Darwin visited the isolated Galapagos Islands and discovered that the animals there were different from the animals elsewhere. Most of them looked like other animals Darwin had seen but they were certainly not the same. After an intensive study of everything there, he suddenly realized that their isolation for so many years meant that they had gradually changed from one generation to the next to now be different. When he reflected on this further he came up with the theory of *natural selection*. This simply means that the need to survive naturally causes those who adapt to the land and the climate the best continue on. It means that those who adapt their own biology and make-up to fit the environment also do better and last longer too. He realized that if you put this theory to work over time, you find the reason that all of life has changed and is changing. He called this theory "evolution", and with it he set off a scientific revolution. Darwin was persecuted by the church and society, thrown out of other scientific circles, and separated from his wife. Still the idea held on and matured, to where it is now see not as a theory but as a fact. There is no more any question to it by educated, sensible, mature people.

We now don't just talk about the evolution of life, but we talk about things like our own evolution and cosmic evolution (with its evolution of galaxies, stars, solar systems, and planets). In science they talk about divergent, convergent, and parallel evolution.

I find the subject of our own evolution to be fascinating because that's what makes up each of our lives. All of us are evolving. We evolve from birth to death; from sleep to activity; from moment to moment, minute to minute, and hour to hour. For instance, when each moment is born and dies within a mini-second, another one is born to live another mini-second and then die. One of the amazing things our brains do is to put this together through our senses to develop our story. Thus thought is also an evolution...and is a most welcome one I might add. I have come to the conclusion that evolution is perhaps the most important discovery that has ever come out of science because it applies to everything. Everything is evolving within us and around us, so the more we can learn about evolution, and grow from it, the better off we'll be.

It is clear that there is forward evolution and backward evolution (which I call de-volution). Obviously evolution is good and devolution is awful. Whenever we are doing anything that obstructs the forward thrust of evolution (coming together), we are devolving and not evolving...we're going backward, We're going against forces such as love and humility (which are a part of The Way) that pull us together.. Thus we see that The Way must be the energy that is behind our forward evolution, and it is the enemy of our devolution. This moral ethic of the cosmos is necessary for reflective evolution to evolve and move forward. Thus The Way is an integral part of all evolution...it is not just connected to our evolution; it is absolutely necessary.

But we've lost it by choosing and evolving into pride rather than humility, and what has that done? Our prideful evolution has made us violent, destructive fools who are killing off ourselves and most other species on the Earth as well. It means we are now *de*volving instead of *e*volving; It means the cosmos is casting us off in its vast evolution because we're pulling it back with our divisions and acts of violence. We have become a deviant evolving species that is one of its reflective-conscious flops. Of course The Way has not left us (because it always been everywhere), but we have left The Way. It appears that we have put it to sleep in us, but it's sill right there. It's waiting to be who we are. We can still correctly evolve into The Way to come together with each other, other species, and with the Earth and cosmos to be lasting and real.

It will never be to late for us to evolve into The Way, but it will soon be too late because we won't be around long enough to do it. We can't control what others do, but we can control what we do.. But is it possible for us to evolve into The Way within such messed-up surroundings? I'm sure that it is because there are those who have done it. They are not waiting for our company, but the fellowship and encouragement of others is always nice. Once again, I'm not trying to start any sort of movement or religion, but I am not against the warmth and friendships that is found in like minded, unselfish gatherings. To come together to form exclusive, prideful groups is very bad, but to evolve in The Way to form inclusive, humble groups paints the future of reflective beings throughout the cosmos. Still each one of us must begin by first seeing and striving to become The Way...it must begin in us. It's up to you and me to reverse this nonsense as we evolve into The Way to start living fully and continuing on as a part of the cosmos' evolution.

APPENDICES V

Extinction

An article from the Washington Post by Kristine Phillips
about a study in the National Academy of Sciences Juournal

Have humans damaged the Earth's ecosystems so severely that we're well on our way to the biggest mass extinction since the dinosaurs vanished 66 million years ago? And are we running out of time to reverse the negative impacts of our actions? Three scientists who have studied extinctions of thousands of species of vertebrates believe so, though others are skeptical of the doomsday-like findings.

A new study published Monday paints a grim picture: The populations of nearly 9,000 vertebrate species, including mammals such as cheetahs, lions and giraffes, have significantly declined between 1900 and 2015. Almost 200 species have gone extinct in the past 100 years alone — a rate of two per year. The study says the losses are indicative of the planet's "ongoing six major extinction events" and has cascading consequences for human life on Earth.

"This is the case of a biological annihilation occurring globally, even if the species these populations belong to are still present somewhere on Earth," Rodolfo Dirzo, the study's co-author and a Stanford University biology professor, said in a news release.

The researchers analyzed 27,600 species of birds, amphibians, mammals and reptiles — about half of all known vertebrate species — and found that 8,851 (about 32 percent) have seen declining populations and shrinking areas of habitat. A more detailed analysis on 177 mammal species found that more than 40 percent have experienced significant drops in population. The findings, the study says, mean that billions of animal populations that once roamed the Earth are now gone. The authors describe the shrinking population of species as "a massive erosion of the greatest biological diversity in the history of Earth."

"Thus, we emphasize that the sixth mass extinction is already here and the window for effective action is very short, probably two or three decades at most," the authors wrote. "All signs point to ever more powerful assaults on biodiversity in the next two decades, painting a dismal picture of the future of life, including human life."

A few examples: There were only a little more than 7,000 cheetahs in existence last year, and their population may drop another 53 percent over the next 15 years, according to National Geographic. Borneo and Sumatran orangutans have been considered endangered for years mainly because of loss of habitat.

The population of African lions has dropped by more than 40 percent in the last 20 years. West African lions, in particular, are nearing extinction, with only about 400 animals left. Historically, lions roamed southern Europe, the Middle East, northwestern India and most of Africa. Today, there are only scattered populations in sub-Saharan Africa and a few remnants at Gir Forest National Park in India, according to the study. The driving force is a steady drumbeat of human activities that result in habitat losses, pollution and climate disruption, among others.

"This is the first mass extinction which the cause knows what it's doing and is harming itself," another co-author, Stanford University biology professor Paul Ehrlich, said. "When the asteroid hit 66 million years ago, the asteroid wasn't making a choice. Now the driver is human overpopulation and over-consumption by the rich, and that's generally accepted." For instance, wildlife habitats have been plowed, paved and replaced with buildings, strip malls and agricultural lands, Ehrlich said.

"The massive loss of populations and species reflects our lack of empathy to all the wild species that have been our companions since our origins," the study's lead author, Gerardo Ceballos, an ecology professor at the Universidad Nacional Autónoma de México, said in the news release. "It is a prelude to the disappearance of many more

177

species and the decline of natural systems that make civilization possible."

Some in the scientific community disagree with the study's grim findings. Doug Erwin, curator at the Smithsonian National Museum of Natural History, said placing the ongoing extinctions of animal species in the same playing field as the mass extinction events in history, or the Big Five, amounts to "junk science."

"Many of those making facile comparisons between the current situation and past mass extinctions don't have a clue about the difference in the nature of the data, much less how truly awful the mass extinctions recorded in the marine fossil record actually were," he told the Atlantic last month. "It is absolutely critical to recognize that I am NOT claiming that humans haven't done great damage to marine and terrestrial, nor that many extinctions have not occurred and more will certainly occur in the near future. But I do think that as scientists we have a responsibility to be accurate about such comparisons."

Stuart Pimm, head of conservation ecology at Duke University in North Carolina, said the study unnecessarily raises alarms by saying the Earth is already in the midst of a cataclysmic event. Pimm believes the sixth mass extinction is just beginning, and not well on its way. "It's a little bit dramatic," Pimm said. "Yes, we are driving species to extinction a thousand times faster than we should. So yes, there is a problem. But on the other hand, telling people that we're all doomed and going to die isn't terribly helpful."

Ehrlich said the point of the research is exactly that — to cause alarm. "I am an alarmist. My colleagues are alarmists. We're alarmed, and we're frightened. And there's no other way to put it," he said. "It's largely a political and economic problem. We have a government that's doing everything they can to push these things in the wrong direction. We have economists who think they can actually grow forever in a finite planet."

Others agree with the authors, saying the study's findings are bleak — and rightfully so. Kieran Suckling, executive director of the Center for Biological Diversity, said the researchers accurately show that population losses are not just confined to a certain geographic area or within certain species of animals. "What they show is it's a mass, global phenomenon," Suckling said. "I think they made the case very strongly that we are right now in the sixth extinction, and if we continue the trend we're on, we're going to be looking at 50 to 75 percent of our species lost over the next hundred years."

Noah Greenwald, endangered species director for the Center for Biological Diversity, agreed with the researchers' conclusion that the window for humans to take action is quickly getting narrow. "The study is right in raising alarm bells … especially with our change in climate," Greenwald said. "We really need to protect as much habitat as we can now. Our population continues to expand, our consumption continues to expand. We're going in the wrong direction, quickly."

The concept of a sixth mass extinction is not new, and the study is not the first to make the case that Earth is already in the middle of it. Two years ago, some of the same researchers argued that species are disappearing at a rate unparalleled since the Cretaceous mass extinction of dinosaurs. The 2015 study found that vertebrate species have been disappearing up to about 100 times the normal rate over the last century.

On a happier note, scientists point to efforts to save endangered species and their habitats

.   "We've dramatically increased the area protected by national parks, increased the area of the oceans that's being protected. We have reduced deforestation rate in the Amazon," Pimm said. "I'm not trying to say that it's all good news, but there's good news out there."

And there's a chance to save endangered species — as long as humans fully commit to it, Suckling said.

"Because once they go on endangered species list, they go from neglect or maybe tacit management to very active, focused efforts to save them. And those work," Suckling said. "The good news here is that once humans decide to save individual species — and we're quite good at it — we can actually reverse this negative trend."

Concerned citizens can do practical things like planting native plans in their yard. They can also contact their representatives in Congress to show their support for habitat protection, Greenwald said, though he cautioned that the current Congress is "the most anti-endangered species in history."

The Center for Biological Diversity has tallied 34 pending bills that would weaken protections for endangered species, Greenwald said.